Carte du Jour
2nd Edition

THE RESTAURANTS OF ROYAL CARIBBEAN INTERNATIONAL

Welcome to *Carte du Jour 2nd Edition*, the newest Royal Caribbean International cookbook creation.

The success of our cookbooks, the *Savor*™ series and the first edition *Carte du Jour*, along with the warm response from you, our valued guests, have inspired us to create a cookbook to accompany our global revitalization effort, *The Royal Advantage Program*. This provides us the unique opportunity of exhibiting our most successful restaurants, which were created on the *Oasis of the Seas* and *Allure of the Seas* and are soon opening on our other ships, assuring that anywhere you sail on Royal Caribbean, you are guaranteed our tradition of culinary excellence.

Each chapter of the book showcases the creativity of Royal Caribbean International's food and beverage team, and features our individual restaurant concepts; focusing on the most popular and successful dishes.

This cookbook is more than just a collection of great recipes; it is a gastronomic journey through Royal Caribbean International's ever-evolving dining experience. It is about the service, wine, cocktails, ambiance, food and most importantly, about what makes our operations and restaurants live and breathe every day.

In the first edition, we touched briefly on the complex process of what it takes to create new dishes and menus for our fleet. In this second edition, we want to highlight the people behind the scenes in our restaurants and galleys.

In *Carte du Jour 2nd Edition*, I would like to take the time to acknowledge our amazing culinary, stewarding, bar and service staff. Those who are on a relentless journey, full of passion and dedication to not only please our guests, but to exceed expectations with every meal they prepare and serve.

To add to the complexity, our staff consists of culinary professionals from 25 different countries working together every day. Every group responds to different styles of motivation, each having their individual talents and driving force. This wonderful team of Commis Cooks, Chef de Parties, Sous Chefs, Executive Sous Chefs, Executive Chefs and our Senior Executive Chefs, along with the corporate office staff, works and supports my efforts at the corporate office to deliver the ultimate guest satisfaction.

In addition, we have Royal Caribbean International's 22 Windjammer buffet restaurants, which are extremely popular for breakfast and lunch, and offer a wide variety of foods in a very casual atmosphere. For further choices, we have 62 optional specialty restaurants ranging from high-end Michelin Star experiences such as our *150 Central Park*, which features an exquisite tasting menu and fine dining; *Izumi*, an Asian-inspired concept; and *Chops Grille*, a sophisticated steak house experience; to intimate restaurant atmospheres like *Samba Grill*, a Churrascaria; *Rita's Cantina*, which offers Mexican-inspired food in a lively atmosphere; and the casual Italian experience at *Giovanni's Table*.

I hope you found this brief insight into our back of house operations of interest.

Carte du Jour 2nd Edition is a compilation of recipes developed with our guests in mind and will hopefully contain a few of your favorites. Browse through the wide variety of offerings and travel the world from the comfort of your very own kitchen, bringing back memories of your cruise vacation experience onboard Royal Caribbean International.

Bon Voyage and Bon Appétit!

Josef Jungwirth

Josef Jungwirth
Director of Fleet Culinary Operations

Welcome to *Carte du Jour 2nd Edition*, the cookbook that introduces you to the signature dishes found in the specialty restaurants onboard Royal Caribbean International's fleet of ships.

Royal Caribbean is committed to delivering an exceptional onboard dining experience by continuously developing innovative programs and upholding the highest of culinary standards. We strive to constantly deliver new and interesting concepts giving our guests the variety and flexibility to meet their evolving tastes and expectations. Within these pages, we present some of the signature dishes served in nine of our popular onboard specialty restaurants, including those aboard our newest addition in the fleet — the world's largest and most innovative cruise ships, *Oasis of the Seas* and *Allure of the Seas*.

At Royal Caribbean, innovation is in our DNA and that extends to include the many dining options we offer aboard our ships. From breakfast to late night snacks, guests can find an extensive variety of food and beverage offerings that will satisfy any craving or personal preferences. At one of our newest and most contemporary dining venues, *150 Central Park*, guests can savor such dishes as *Camembert and Lager Soup*, or *Corn Nut Crusted Halibut with Sorrel Pudding*. They also can experience a family-style feast influenced by the Tuscan countryside of Italy at *Giovanni's Table*, or be transported to Brazil at *Samba Grill*, our Churrascaria-style Brazilian restaurant. If guests are looking for something a little lighter, enjoy the *Assorted Sushi Rolls* offered in the Asian bistro, *Izumi*.

While the dishes featured within this book may at first seem daunting to prepare, all recipes are delivered in a simple and straightforward fashion with ingredients and equipment that are readily available. With a tempting selection of dishes, *Carte du Jour 2nd Edition* will inspire you to come back to enjoy your Royal Caribbean cruise vacation experience over and over again.

What's more, a portion of the proceeds of your *Carte du Jour* cookbook purchase will benefit *Big Brothers and Big Sisters of Greater Miami*, a volunteer-supported program helping at-risk children succeed through adult mentor relationships.

Thank you for your support and bon appétit!

Adam M. Goldstein

Adam Goldstein
President
Royal Caribbean International

GIOVANNI'S TABLE

IZUMI

SAMBA GRILL

CHEF'S TABLE

VINTAGES

150 CENTRAL PARK

Table of Contents

RITA'S CANTINA

CHOPS GRILLE

DINING ROOM

Carte du Jour
2nd Edition

Josef Jungwirth, Director of Fleet Culinary Operations

With 10,000 crystal elements, a height of 18 feet (5.50 meters), a diameter of 10.5 feet (3.20 meters), and a weight of 2,095 pounds (950 kg), the main chandelier sets the tone with an elegant, expansive grandeur, a gilded design and an Art Deco touch.

The main mural, which was first mapped out in detail in small-scale paintings, was later painted in 3 segments, each taking approximately 2 months to complete, featuring a center figure over 9 feet tall.

Share a classic meal with family or friends. Each dish is prepared with our talented chefs' own special twists. Choose a wine from our extensive wine list and allow us to pamper you.

The Dining Rooms onboard Royal Caribbean International bring to mind an earlier time, when transatlantic crossings were the civilized way to journey between continents. We have updated the experience with all the conveniences of this century, such as "My Time Dining", allowing you, our guests, the flexibility to dine at your leisure throughout your voyage.

Dining Room

Oakwood Smoked Chicken Breast Salad

DRESSING
1/3 cup (85 g) blue cheese
3 tablespoons (45 g) buttermilk
3 tablespoons (45 g) sour cream
2 tablespoons (30 g) mayonnaise
1 teaspoon (5 ml) white wine vinegar
1 teaspoon (5 ml) freshly squeezed
lemon juice
1/2 teaspoon (2.5 g) granulated sugar
1/8 teaspoon (0.5 g) garlic powder
1/8 bunch fresh chives, chopped
Salt and freshly ground black pepper

SALAD
1 head Boston lettuce, washed
3 green apples, cored, quartered,
sliced and kept in cold water mixed with
1 tablespoon (15 ml) lemon juice
2 12 to 16-ounce (340 g to 453 g) smoked
chicken breasts, purchased, sliced crosswise
into 1-ounce (30 g) slices
1/2 pound (250 g) carrots, peeled and julienned
1/2 pound (250 g) celeriac, peeled and julienned
1/4 pound (125 g) snow peas,
blanched and julienned
1/4 pound (125 g) alfalfa sprouts

GARNISH
1/2 pound (250 g) seedless red grapes, halved
1/2 cup (115 g) walnuts, toasted on a cookie sheet

EQUIPMENT
Chef's knives and cutting board
Cookie sheet
Fork
Glass or stainless steel bowl

To make the dressing, mash blue cheese and buttermilk together with a fork in a small glass bowl until the mixture resembles cottage cheese. Stir in remaining ingredients and season with salt and pepper to taste. Cover and refrigerate.

Place Boston lettuce leaves on six chilled plates. Arrange several layers of apple slices, smoked chicken and vegetable julienne.

Top salads with remaining vegetable julienne and small bunches of alfalfa sprouts.

Garnish with grapes and toasted walnuts.

Drizzle with blue cheese dressing.

Serves 6.

Difficulty 1.

Dining Room

WINE PAIRING ⌘ MACMURRAY RANCH, PINOT GRIS, SONOMA COAST, CALIFORNIA

Pan-Seared Crusted Sea Scallops

ONION CONFIT
1/2 head of garlic, peeled and shaved
2 medium onions, peeled and shaved
1/3 cup (90 ml) extra virgin olive oil

CAULIFLOWER PURÉE
1/2 cauliflower, florets only, chopped
1 clove garlic, peeled and crushed
1 cup (240 ml) cold water
1 teaspoon (15 g) sea salt
1 tablespoon (15 g) salted butter
1 tablespoon (15 g) sour cream
2 tablespoons (30 ml) heavy cream
Pinch of ground nutmeg
Salt and freshly ground white pepper

CRUMBS
4 ounces (120 g) sliced prosciutto, thinly chopped
1/3 cup (85 g) panko breadcrumbs
1 teaspoon (5 g) lemon zest, finely chopped
1 teaspoon finely chopped fresh thyme
1 teaspoon finely chopped chives

SCALLOPS
12 sea scallops
Salt and freshly ground white pepper

CHORIZO
1 spicy Spanish chorizo, sliced

EQUIPMENT
2 small saucepans
Chef's knives and cutting board
Colander
Food processor
Large glass bowl
Large pot
Large sauté pans
Ovenproof dish
Paper towels
Small glass bowl
Small sauté pan
Wooden spoon

Preheat oven to 355°F or 180°C.

For the onion confit, simmer garlic and onions in olive oil in a small saucepan over medium heat for 20 minutes. Do not brown. Allow to cool. Cover and reserve.

To make cauliflower purée, cook cauliflower florets and garlic in a pot of salted water. Bring to a boil, add butter and cook for 10 minutes or until cauliflower is easily pierced with the tip of a knife. Drain cauliflower using a colander and transfer into a food processor.

Add remaining ingredients and purée until smooth. Season with salt and pepper to taste.

Set aside in a glass bowl and keep warm.

While cauliflower is cooking, warm 2 tablespoons (30 ml) of onion confit in a small saucepan over medium-high heat, and sauté for 2 minutes. Add prosciutto and cook for 6 to 7 minutes or until crispy. Transfer into a small glass bowl and mix with panko breadcrumbs, lemon zest, thyme and chives. Set aside and keep warm.

Pat dry scallops with paper towels and season them with salt and pepper.

Warm 1 tablespoon (15 ml) onion confit in a large sauté pan over medium-high heat and sear scallops for 1 minute on both sides. Remove scallops from pan and place in an ovenproof dish.

Sprinkle scallops with panko mixture and bake for 2 minutes.

Meanwhile, warm 1 tablespoon (15 ml) onion confit in a small sauté pan over medium heat. Place chorizo slices in the pan and sauté for 4 minutes, turning often.

Arrange a spoonful of cauliflower purée on a warm appetizer dish and pull in a left to right motion to create an elongated line across the plate. Top with 2 seared scallops and a couple of sautéed chorizo slices.

Serves 6.

Difficulty 1.

Dining Room

Chilled Soup Duo

SUGAR SYRUP
1/2 cup (115 g) granulated sugar
1/2 cup (120 ml) water

BERRY FRAPPÉ
1 1/2 cups (350 g) fresh strawberries
1 cup (235 g) frozen strawberries
1/2 cup (115 g) fresh raspberries
1/4 cup (60 g) fresh blueberries
1 teaspoon (5 ml) lemon juice
1 cup (235 g) raspberry sherbet, purchased
3 tablespoons (45 ml) sugar syrup

PINEAPPLE LYCHEE BISQUE
1 ripe pineapple, peeled,
stalk removed and diced small
1 20-ounce (565 g) can of lychee
in liquid, drained
1/4 cup (60 ml) sugar syrup
Juice of 1 freshly squeezed lemon
3 tablespoons (45 ml) Malibu liquor

CREAM
1/2 cup (120 ml) heavy cream
2 tablespoons (30 ml) Malibu liquor

GARNISH
Coconut shavings, lightly toasted
in the oven on a cookie sheet
Mint leaves

EQUIPMENT
2 glass bowls
Blender
Chef's knives and cutting board
Cookie sheet
Handheld mixer
Saucepan
Toothpick

To make syrup, place sugar and water in a small saucepan and simmer over medium heat until sugar has completely dissolved. Pour syrup into an airtight container and refrigerate. Sugar syrup can be kept in the fridge for several weeks.

Make berry frappé by placing all the ingredients in a blender or food processor. Blend until smooth and transfer to a chilled glass bowl. Cover with plastic wrap and refrigerate.

For pineapple lychee bisque, place all the ingredients in a blender and blend until smooth. Transfer bisque into a chilled glass bowl, cover with plastic wrap and refrigerate for at least 3 hours.

Just before serving, place half of the heavy cream in a chilled glass bowl. Add Malibu liquor and beat at medium-high speed with a handheld mixer, until soft peaks form.

Pour chilled soups into individual serving glasses.

Add a few drops of heavy cream into the berry frappé and using a toothpick, create a cream swirl.

Place a dollop of Malibu whipped cream on the pineapple lychee bisque. Garnish with toasted coconut shavings and mint leaves.

Serves 6.

Difficulty 1.

WINE PAIRING ❧ CAPOSALDO, PROSECCO, BRUT, VENETO, ITALY

Dining Room

WINE PAIRING ᕧ ALBARIÑO PACO & LOLA, RÍAS BAIXAS, SPAIN

Fish Chowder

SEMI DRIED TOMATOES

6 Roma tomatoes, halved
1/4 cup (60 ml) extra virgin olive oil
Salt and freshly ground black pepper

CHOWDER

2 tablespoons (30 g) salted butter
1 tablespoon (15 ml) extra virgin olive oil
1 large yellow onion, peeled and finely diced
1 stalk celery, finely diced
1/2 red bell pepper, diced small
1/2 green bell pepper, diced small
2 cloves garlic, peeled and diced
2 bay leaves
1/2 teaspoon (2.5 g) celery salt
2 whole allspice cloves
1 whole clove
1/8 bunch fresh cilantro
2 cups (480 ml) fish stock (page 156)

2 large Yukon Gold potatoes, peeled, cut in
1/2-inch (1.2 cm) cubes and kept in a large bowl
filled with cold water
1/4 cup (60 ml) heavy cream
1/2 pound (250 g) salmon fillet,
skinless and cubed
1/2 pound (250 g) 21/25 raw shrimp,
peeled and deveined
1/2 pound (250 g) mussels, steamed
and removed from the shell
1/2 pound (250 g) corvina fillet,
skinless and cubed
Salt and freshly ground black pepper

GARNISH

1/4 bunch parsley

EQUIPMENT

Baking sheet
Blender
Chef's knife and cutting board
Ladle
Large stockpot
Parchment paper
Wooden spoon

Preheat oven to 260°F or 126°C.

Lay tomatoes face up on a baking sheet lined with parchment paper. Drizzle with olive oil and season with salt and pepper. Place in the oven and bake for 10 minutes or until tomatoes are semi dried (slightly shrunken but still soft).

To make the chowder, warm butter and olive oil in a large stockpot over medium heat. Add onions, celery, bell peppers and garlic and sauté for 4 to 5 minutes or until onion is translucent. Do not brown. Add bay leaves, celery salt, allspice cloves, whole clove and cilantro.

Add fish stock a little at a time, stirring constantly with a wooden spoon. Incorporate potatoes and semi dried tomatoes and stir well. Bring to a boil.

Reduce heat and simmer 10 to 12 minutes or until potatoes are tender.

Remove a small amount of cooked vegetables from the chowder and set aside.

Remove bay leaves and discard.

Pour chowder in a blender and process until smooth. Transfer back in the stockpot. Bring to a simmer over low heat. Whisk in heavy cream.

Add fish, seafood and reserved vegetables back to the chowder and simmer for another 3 to 4 minutes or until fish is cooked throughout, stirring occasionally.

Season to taste with salt and freshly ground black pepper.

Ladle soup into warmed bowls and garnish with fresh parsley.

Serves 6.

Difficulty 1.

Kummelweck Sandwich

STRIP LOIN

1 3 to 4-pound (1.3 kg to 1.8 kg) boneless beef strip loin
Salt and freshly ground black pepper
3 tablespoons (45 ml) extra virgin olive oil

SPICY MUSTARD

1/2 cup (115 g) Gulden's spicy brown mustard
1 medium yellow onion, peeled and diced
1/2 red bell pepper, diced
1/2 green bell pepper, diced
1 pickle, diced
1 tablespoon (15 g) prepared horseradish
1 teaspoon (5 ml) Worcestershire sauce
2 teaspoons (10 ml) A1 sauce

AU JUS

1/4 cup (60 ml) red wine
1 cup (240 ml) beef stock (page 157)

POTATO CHIPS

1 cup (240 ml) vegetable oil
3 Yukon Gold potatoes, peeled and thinly sliced with a mandolin
Sea salt
1/4 bunch parsley, chopped

SANDWICH

8 bread buns, purchased, sliced in the middle
1 seedless English cucumber, peeled and quartered
Grated horseradish sauce

EQUIPMENT

Aluminum foil
Carving knife, Chef's knives and cutting board
Fine sieve
Mandolin
Metal tongs
Paper towels
Roasting pan
Shallow pan
Slotted spoon
Small glass bowl
Small ladle
Small saucepan
Small whisk
Wooden spoon

Preheat oven to 350°F or 176°C.

Pat beef strip loin dry with paper towels. Season with salt and pepper on all sides and rub with olive oil. Place meat fat side up in a roasting pan and sear over high heat, on all sides for 5 to 7 minutes. Roast meat in the oven for about 35 minutes or until a thermometer inserted in the center of the meat registers a temperature of 120°F or 48°C for medium rare. If you prefer beef cooked to medium doneness, roast for an additional 5 to 7 minutes to bring the temperature to 140°F or 60°C.

Remove pan from the oven and tent with aluminum foil. Let rest for 15 minutes.

To make spicy mustard, combine all ingredients in a small glass bowl and mix well. Cover and refrigerate.

Transfer roast onto a carving surface or cutting board and slice crosswise into 1/3-inch (0.8 cm) thick slices.

For au jus, place roasting pan on the stove burner set on high heat. Add wine to the pan and cook for 2 minutes, scraping the drippings from the bottom of the pan. Add beef stock and bring to a boil. Reduce heat and simmer for about 10 minutes or until liquid has reduced by half. Skim the surface of the remaining liquid to remove excess fat. Strain liquid through a fine sieve into a small saucepan and set aside.

For potato chips, place oil in a shallow pan over high heat. Pat potatoes dry and fry in hot oil in batches, stirring often with metal tongs for about 5 minutes or until potatoes are golden. Remove from oil with a slotted spoon and place on a large platter covered with paper towels. Season with sea salt and toss with chopped parsley.

Build each sandwich by placing a couple spoonfuls of au jus on the bottom part of the bun. Layer with slices of roast beef and top with a small spoonful of spicy mustard and a touch of horseradish.

Place sandwich on a warm plate. Serve with potato chips and cucumber slices, accompanied by separate dishes of grated horseradish, spicy mustard and au jus.

Serves 8.

Difficulty 1.

Black and Tan

1 part Bass® pale ale
1 part Guinness® stout

Fill chilled stein glass half full with Bass® then slowly pour Guinness® over a spoon until glass is full.

Dining Room

WINE PAIRING ✑ BELLE GLOS, PINOT NOIR BLANC, "OEIL DE PERDRIX", YORKVILLE HIGHLANDS, CALIFORNIA

Artichoke Crêpes au Gratin

ONION CONFIT
1/2 head of garlic, peeled and shaved
2 medium onions, peeled and shaved
1/3 cup (90 ml) extra virgin olive oil

CRÊPES
1 cup (235 g) all-purpose flour
1/4 teaspoon (1 g) salt
2 eggs
1 cup (240 ml) milk
2 tablespoons (30 g) salted butter, melted

WHITE SAUCE
2 tablespoons (30 g) salted butter
2 tablespoons (30 g) all-purpose flour
1/4 teaspoon (1 g) ground nutmeg
1 cup (240 ml) milk
Salt and freshly ground black pepper

ARTICHOKES
6 tablespoons (90 ml) onion confit
1 pound (450 g) frozen artichoke hearts, defrosted
3 tablespoons (45 ml) dry white wine
Salt and freshly ground black pepper

ARTICHOKE CHEESE FILLING
3 tablespoons (45 ml) onion confit
3/4 cup (175 g) ricotta cheese
1/2 cup (115 g) shredded Gruyère cheese
1/4 cup (60 g) grated Parmesan cheese

GARNISH
3 to 4 artichoke hearts (canned), trimmed, each leaf separated
1 tablespoon (15 ml) extra virgin olive oil
Salt
1/4 bunch of parsley, chopped
1/2 red bell pepper, julienned
Parmesan shavings
Fresh basil

EQUIPMENT
2 small saucepans
Baking dish
Chef's knives and cutting board
Glass or stainless steel bowl
Griddle or frying pan
Large saucepan
Medium saucepan
Medium sauté pan
Parchment paper
Silpat or cookie sheet
Spatula
Wire whisk

Preheat oven to 320°F or 160°C.

For the onion confit, simmer garlic and onions in olive oil in a small saucepan over medium heat for 20 minutes. Do not brown. Allow to cool. Cover and reserve.

While confit is simmering, place artichoke leaves for garnish on a Silpat or a cookie sheet covered with parchment paper. Rub olive oil into the leaves and season with salt. Dry leaves in the oven for 15 to 20 minutes or until they are slightly golden around the edges.

To make the crêpes, place flour, salt and eggs in a glass or stainless steel bowl and whisk together using a wire whisk.

Add milk gradually, whisking constantly.

Melt butter in a small saucepan over medium heat and fold into crêpe batter.

Heat a griddle or frying pan over medium-high heat and oil lightly. Using a small ladle, pour batter onto the griddle or pan, gently tilting it in a circular motion to coat the pan evenly.

Cook crêpe for about 1 to 1 1/2 minutes or until the edges turn light brown. Gently loosen crêpe with a spatula, flip and cook the other side for about 1 minute. Stack crêpes on a warm dish.

Repeat until all the batter has been used, for a total of 12 to 14 crêpes.

For white sauce, melt butter in a small saucepan over medium heat. Add flour and nutmeg and stir with a wooden spoon until well incorporated. Add milk a little at a time, stirring constantly until the sauce thickens. Season with salt and pepper. Keep warm.

To prepare the artichokes, heat onion confit in a sauté pan over medium-high heat. Add artichoke hearts and sauté for 5 minutes, stirring often. Deglaze with white wine, season with salt and pepper and cook at medium heat for another 5 minutes or until artichokes are cooked through.

To make the filling, heat onion confit in a large saucepan over medium heat. Add ricotta and cook for 3 to 4 minutes or until melted and smooth, stirring often.

Add Gruyère and most of the Parmesan cheese and mix well. Remove from heat and stir in sautéed artichokes.

Lay crêpes on a clean work surface. Place a couple of spoonfuls of artichoke cheese mixture in the center of each crêpe and roll up loosely. Place filled crêpes in a baking dish, cover with white sauce and dust with remaining Parmesan cheese.

Bake for 10 to 15 minutes or until Parmesan cheese crust is golden.

Using a spatula, carefully remove two crêpes at a time from the baking dish and arrange them on warm plates. Sprinkle with chopped parsley and a few dried artichoke leaves.

Garnish with julienne red pepper, Parmesan shavings and fresh basil.

Serves 6.

Difficulty 2.

Horseradish Crusted Salmon

CELERIAC-POTATO MASH

1 1/2 pounds (700 g) celeriac,
peeled and chopped
1 cup (240 ml) milk
5 cups (1.2 L) cold water
1 teaspoon (5 g) sea salt
2 bay leaves

1 pound (450 g) Yukon Gold potatoes,
peeled and quartered
3 cups (720 ml) cold water
1 teaspoon (5 g) sea salt
3/4 cup (180 ml) heavy cream
3 tablespoons (45 g) unsalted butter
1 tablespoon (15 g) grated horseradish
Salt and freshly ground white pepper

DILLED CUCUMBER

1 seedless English cucumber, peeled and
julienned
1/4 bunch fresh dill, chopped
Juice of 1 freshly squeezed lemon
1 teaspoon (5 g) granulated sugar
1 teaspoon (5 ml) extra virgin olive oil
Pinch of salt

FISH

2 tablespoons (30 g) chopped parsley
2 tablespoons (30 g) chopped chives
2 tablespoons (30 g) grated horseradish,
purchased in a jar
1/2 cup (115 g) panko breadcrumbs
6 6-ounce (170 g) salmon medallions
Salt and freshly ground black pepper
1/4 cup (60 g) Dijon mustard
2 tablespoons (30 ml) vegetable oil

LEMON BEURRE BLANC

1 shallot, peeled and minced
3 tablespoons (45 ml) brandy
3/4 cup (180 ml) fish stock (page 156)
Juice of 1 freshly squeezed lemon
1/2 pound (250 g) cubed, unsalted cold butter
Salt and freshly ground white pepper

MUSTARD SAUCE

2 tablespoons (30 g) honey
2 tablespoons (30 g) Dijon mustard
3 tablespoons (45 ml) Champagne

VEGETABLES

4 ounces (120 g) snow peas, blanched

GARNISH

1/4 bunch fresh dill, dusted with all-purpose
flour and fried until crispy

EQUIPMENT

2 small glass or stainless steel bowls
2 small saucepans
Brush
Chef's knives and cutting board
Colander
Food processor
Heavy sauté pan
Large glass bowls
Large pot
Large sauté pan
Ovenproof skillet
Paper towels
Potato ricer
Sieve
Wire whisk
Wooden spoon

Preheat oven to 320°F or 160°C.

To make celeriac-potato mash, place celeriac in a pot of salted milk, water and bay leaves. Bring to a boil and cook for 20 minutes over medium-high heat or until celeriac is easily pierced with the tip of a knife. Remove bay leaves, drain celeriac using a colander and press through a potato ricer into a heated bowl.

For mashed potatoes, place potatoes into salted cold water, bring to a boil and cook until potatoes are easily pierced with the tip of a knife, about 15 minutes. Drain potatoes using a colander and press through a potato ricer into the bowl already containing the celeriac. Stir in cream, butter and horseradish. Adjust seasoning with salt and pepper. Set aside and keep warm.

While celeriac and potatoes are cooking, place julienned cucumbers and remaining ingredients in a small glass or stainless steel bowl. Mix well. Cover and refrigerate.

To make salmon crust, place parsley, chives, horseradish and panko breadcrumbs in a food processor and blend until very fine.

Pat salmon medallions dry with paper towels and season both sides with salt and pepper. Brush the top of each medallion with Dijon mustard, then press panko mixture on with your hands.

Heat oil in a large sauté pan over medium-high heat and sear medallions on both sides for 2 minutes. Transfer into an ovenproof dish and bake for 6 minutes.

To make the lemon beurre blanc, melt 1 teaspoon (5 g) of the butter in a sauté pan over medium heat. Add shallots and sauté for 2 minutes. Deglaze the pan with brandy, add fish stock and lemon juice and bring to a boil. Reduce heat and simmer for 6 minutes or until mixture has reduced by half. Remove pan from heat and whisk in butter a little at a time. Strain sauce through a sieve and adjust seasoning to taste with salt and pepper.

Make the mustard sauce by mixing all ingredients together in a small bowl and store in an airtight container. This sauce can be prepared several days in advance.

To serve, place a spoonful of celeriac-potato mash in the center of a warm entrée plate and top with a salmon medallion. Drizzle with lemon beurre blanc and a little mustard sauce. Artfully arrange a few snow peas on the plate and crown each medallion with dilled cucumber julienne and fried dill.

Serves 6.

Difficulty 3.

WINE PAIRING ❦ HARTFORD COURT, CHARDONNAY, "STONE CÔTE VINEYARD", SONOMA COAST, USA

Dining Room

Veal Scallopini Oscar

MASHED POTATOES

2 pounds (900 g) Yukon Gold potatoes,
peeled and quartered
6 cups (1.4 L) cold water
1 teaspoon (5 g) sea salt
3/4 cup (180 ml) heavy cream
2 tablespoons (30 g) unsalted butter
Salt and freshly ground white pepper

HOLLANDAISE SAUCE

4 egg yolks
Juice of 1 freshly squeezed lemon
Pinch of freshly ground white pepper
1 tablespoon (15 ml) water
1 cup (235 g) butter, melted
1/4 teaspoon (1 g) salt

WHITE SAUCE

2 tablespoons (30 g) butter
2 tablespoons (30 g) all-purpose flour
1 cup (240 ml) milk
Salt and freshly ground black pepper
Pinch of ground nutmeg
3/4 pound (375 g) lump crab meat
3 tablespoons (45 g) grated Parmesan cheese

VEAL SCALLOPINI

12 3-ounce (85 g) veal scallopini (cutlets),
pounded thin
Salt and freshly ground black pepper
1/4 cup (60 g) all-purpose flour
2 tablespoons (30 ml) extra virgin olive oil
1/3 cup (90 ml) dry white wine
1 cup (240 ml) demi-glace (page 157)

VEGETABLES

12 green asparagus spears, peeled,
trimmed and blanched
3 tomatoes, halved, seasoned and grilled

GARNISH

Chopped parsley

EQUIPMENT

2 medium glass bowls
2 small saucepans
Chef's knives and cutting board
Colander
Large pot
Large sauté pan
Medium saucepan
Paper towels
Platter
Potato ricer
Wire whisk

Preheat oven to 320°F or 160°C.

For mashed potatoes, place potatoes into a pot filled with salted cold water. Bring to a boil and cook until potatoes are easily pierced with the tip of a knife, about 15 minutes. Drain potatoes using a colander and press potatoes through a potato ricer into a heated bowl. Stir in cream and butter. Adjust seasoning with salt and pepper. Set aside and keep warm.

For hollandaise, fill the bottom of a medium-sized saucepan with water. Place glass bowl over a double boiler of simmering water, making sure there is no contact between the bowl and the water.

Place eggs in the glass bowl and whisk with lemon juice, pepper and water.

Slowly add melted butter to egg mixture, whisking constantly. Remove bowl from heat. Whisk in salt. Cover and keep warm.

To make white sauce, melt butter in a small saucepan over medium heat. Add flour and stir until flour and butter are well combined. Pour in milk, stirring constantly as it thickens. Season with salt, pepper and nutmeg. Remove from heat and set aside.

Warm crab meat in a small saucepan over low heat.

Mix warmed crab meat with white sauce. Add grated Parmesan and season with salt and pepper.

Pat veal scallopini dry with paper towels and season them with salt and pepper. Place flour in a glass bowl. Dredge veal scallopini in flour, shaking off the excess.

Warm olive oil in a large sauté pan over medium-high heat and sear veal for 1 minute on each side. Remove from pan and transfer to a platter.

Deglaze pan with white wine, then add demi-glace. Simmer for 5 minutes. Taste sauce and adjust seasoning with salt and pepper to taste. Keep warm.

Place 2 tablespoons of crab mixture on top of each veal scallopini. Place in the oven for 5 minutes or until heated throughout.

Arrange a tomato on a warmed entrée plate. Place a mound of mashed potatoes in the center of the plate, top with the veal scallopini and crisscross with two or three asparagus spears. Drizzle with hollandaise sauce and veal sauce.

Sprinkle with chopped parsley.

Serves 6.

Difficulty 4.

Potato, Leek and Spinach Mille-Feuille

MILLE-FEUILLE

1 tablespoon (15 ml) extra virgin olive oil
2/3 cup (140 g) salted butter
2 leeks, washed and thinly sliced,
white part only
3/4 pound (375 g) fresh spinach,
washed and chopped
2 cloves garlic, peeled and finely chopped
4 pounds (1.8 kg) Kipfler or
red skin potatoes, peeled
3 1/2 cups (840 ml) heavy cream
2/3 cup (140 g) panko breadcrumbs
Zest of 1 lemon
Salt and freshly ground black pepper

RED PEPPER COULIS

4 red bell peppers
1 tablespoon (15 ml) extra virgin olive oil
Salt and freshly ground black pepper

GARNISH

1 fennel bulb, washed, thinly sliced
and kept in a bowl of ice water
1/2 cup (115 g) shredded red cabbage,
kept in a bowl of ice water
1/2 bunch dill, kept in a bowl of cold water

EQUIPMENT

9" x 13" (23 x 33 cm) pan or baking dish
Blender
Chef's knives and cutting board
Colander
Large glass or stainless steel bowl
Mandolin
Medium glass or stainless steel bowl
Medium saucepan
Round cookie cutter
Sauté pan
Skewer
Small pot
Wooden spoon

Preheat oven to 355°F or 180°C.

Heat oil and 2 tablespoons (30 g) butter in a medium saucepan over medium-high heat until butter is foaming. Add leeks, spinach and garlic and sauté for 3 minutes or until spinach is wilted, stirring occasionally. Season with salt and pepper. Transfer vegetables into a colander and gently press to drain off the excess liquid.

Using the thin-cut setting on a mandolin, slice the potatoes and place them in a large glass or stainless steel bowl filled with heavy cream to prevent discoloration.

Grease a 9" x 13" pan or baking dish with butter and evenly spread the spinach leek mixture on the bottom. Arrange one layer of potatoes on top, allowing the slices to overlap, then season with salt and pepper. Repeat until you have used up all the potato slices. Cover with heavy cream. Dot with 2 tablespoons (30 g) of butter. Bake for 10 minutes.

Melt remaining butter in a small sauté pan over medium heat.

Combine panko breadcrumbs, lemon zest, melted butter and seasoning in a glass or stainless steel bowl and mix well. Remove vegetable dish from the oven and spread the top with the breadcrumb mixture. Return dish to the oven and bake for another 30 to 40 minutes or until potatoes are tender when pierced with a skewer.

While mille-feuille is cooking, make the red bell pepper coulis. Blanch peppers in a small pot filled with boiling water for 5 minutes. Cool peppers in a large glass bowl filled with ice water. Remove skin, stems and seeds from the peppers and place into a blender. Add olive oil and seasoning and blend until smooth.

Once mille-feuille has finished baking, remove from oven and let stand for 5 minutes. Cut mille-feuille into portions using a round cookie cutter.

Place a serving of mille-feuille in the center of a warm entrée plate and top with some fennel, cabbage and dill.

Drizzle red pepper coulis around the mille-feuille and serve.

Serves 6.

Difficulty 2.

Wine Pairing ❧ Penfolds, Pinot Noir, "Cellar Reserve", Australia

Dining Room

WINE PAIRING ⟳ MASSOLINO, MOSCATO D'ASTI, PIEDMONT, ITALY

Sky High Lemon Meringue Tartlets

CRUST
2 cups (465 g) all-purpose flour
Pinch of salt
1 tablespoon (15 g) granulated sugar
1 egg, lightly beaten
3/4 cup (175 g) cold unsalted butter,
   cut into small cubes
1/4 cup (60 ml) cold water

LEMON CREAM
2 whole eggs
2 egg yolks
1/2 cup (120 ml) freshly squeezed lemon juice
1 cup (235 g) granulated sugar
1/2 teaspoon (2.5 ml) lemon extract
4 tablespoons (60 g) unsalted butter
1 tablespoon (15 g) lemon zest

MERINGUE
3 egg whites, room temperature
1/4 teaspoon (2.5 g) cream of tartar
Pinch of salt
1 teaspoon (5 g) lemon zest
1/2 cup (115 g) granulated sugar

GARNISH
Mint leaves
Chocolate cigarettes, purchased

EQUIPMENT
6 4-inch (10 cm) diameter
   individual tart pans
Baking sheet
Cookie cutter
Copper or stainless steel bowl
Electric mixer
Food processor
Fork
Medium round piping tip
Piping or pastry bag or
   plastic sandwich bag
Rolling pin
Small saucepan
Wire rack
Wire whisk

Preheat oven to 355°F or 180°C.

To make the crust, combine flour, salt, sugar and egg in a food processor fitted with a flat blade. Add butter and blend for 3 to 4 minutes or until butter is completely incorporated. Add water 1 tablespoon (15 ml) at a time until mixture clumps together.

Flatten dough into a disk, wrap in plastic wrap and refrigerate for 30 minutes.

Grease tart pans.

Lightly flour work surface and roll dough into a 1/8-inch (3 mm) thick circle. Cut the dough into circles using a cookie cutter about 1 inch (2.5 cm) larger than tart pans. Lay crusts into tart pans and, using your thumb, lightly press into the bottom and sides of the pans. Roll a rolling pin over the top of each pan to get rid of the excess pastry. Prick the bottoms with a fork to keep dough from puffing. Line each tart shell with aluminum foil and refrigerate for 30 minutes.

Fill the foil-lined tart shells with dried beans just before baking (to prevent puffing). Par-bake for 10 minutes then remove beans and aluminum foil. Bake for another 8 to 10 minutes or until tartlet shells are a light gold color.

Remove pans from oven and allow to cool on a wire rack.

To make the filling, mix all the ingredients for the lemon cream in a medium saucepan and bring to a boil. Reduce heat and simmer for 5 minutes, whisking continuously. Remove tartlet shells from the tart pans. Pour lemon mixture into tartlet shells and set aside.

To make the meringue, combine the egg whites, cream of tartar, salt and lemon zest in either a copper or stainless steel bowl. Beat for 3 minutes with an electric mixer on medium-high speed until soft peaks form. Add 1/3 of the sugar and beat for 1 minute only. Repeat two more times until all the sugar has been incorporated. Do not over-beat the meringue or the mixture will separate.

Increase the oven temperature to 450°F or 230°C.

Spoon the meringue egg mixture into a piping or pastry bag or plastic sandwich bag fitted with a medium round tip. Pipe a small amount of meringue into the center of each tartlet for support, then add in long upward strokes, in a smooth bottom-to-top motion.

Transfer tartlets to a baking sheet. Place in oven, leaving the door ajar, and bake for 3 minutes or until the edges of the meringue are golden.

Garnish each tartlet with mint leaves and a chocolate cigarette.

Serves 6.

Difficulty 3.

Chocolate Soufflé

GANACHE
1/2 cup (115 g) dark chocolate
2 tablespoons (30 g) unsalted butter
1/2 cup (120 ml) heavy cream

SOUFFLÉ
1 1/4 cups (300 ml) whole milk
1/2 cup (120 g) granulated sugar
5 tablespoons (100 g) unsalted butter
1/2 cup (120 g) all-purpose flour
6 egg yolks
1/2 cup (115 g) chocolate ganache
2 tablespoons (30 g) cocoa powder
6 egg whites
Pinch of salt
1/4 cup (60 g) sugar

CHOCOLATE ESPRESSO SAUCE
1/4 cup (60 ml) heavy cream
1/4 cup (60 ml) strong espresso
2 tablespoons (30 ml) coffee liqueur

GARNISH
1/4 cup (60 g) powdered sugar
White chocolate accent pieces, purchased

EQUIPMENT
2 small saucepans
4 ovenproof ramekins measuring
4.5-inches (11.5 cm) in diameter
and 2-inches (5 cm) deep
Electric mixer
Medium saucepan
Mixing bowl
Wire whisk
Wooden spoon

Preheat oven to 340°F or 170°C.

To make chocolate ganache, place all ingredients in a small saucepan and slowly warm over low heat until chocolate has melted, stirring often. Remove from heat and set aside.

Butter soufflé dishes or ramekins and dust with a little sugar. Tilt and tap out excess.

Combine milk and sugar in a saucepan and bring to a boil.

For soufflé, melt butter in a medium-sized saucepan over medium heat and slowly whisk in flour. Add milk mixture a little at a time, whisking constantly. Reduce heat to low and slowly cook until mixture pulls away from the side of the saucepan, about 8 to 10 minutes. Do not boil.

Remove from heat and slowly fold in egg yolks, one at a time. Stir in the chocolate ganache and cocoa powder and mix well.

Place egg whites and salt in a mixing bowl and beat with an electric mixer set on medium speed until eggs are frothy. Increase speed to high and gradually add sugar, beating egg whites until they form soft peaks.

Spoon 1/3 of egg whites into the chocolate mixture and very gently mix with a wooden spoon until the batter has lightened. Fold in the remaining egg whites, taking care not to deflate them. Divide the mixture into the soufflé dishes.

Bake for about 20 minutes or until the soufflés have doubled in size and are nicely browned. Remove from the oven and place on a wire rack.

Prepare chocolate sauce while soufflés are baking. Place heavy cream and espresso in a small saucepan over low heat. Slowly whisk in remaining chocolate ganache and coffee liqueur. Remove from heat and pour into a gooseneck serving dish.

Dust soufflés with powdered sugar. Top with a white chocolate accent piece and serve immediately with the chocolate espresso sauce.

Serves 4.

Difficulty 4.

Toasted Almond Kahlúa

1 1/2 oz. (4.5 cl) Kahlúa
1 oz. (3 cl) Amaretto Disaronno Originale
1 1/2 oz. (4.5 cl) half & half

Fill shaker with ice and add all ingredients. Shake well and strain into an ice filled rock glass.

WINE PAIRING ⌒ BODEGAS BORSAO, CAMPO DE BORJA, SPAIN

Dining Room

This colorful and lively restaurant specializes in classic Mexican fare and Tex-Mex favorites in a relaxed, informal setting. An outdoor seating area opens onto the Boardwalk, and is much in demand by guests who love people watching while enjoying a refreshing margarita from the largest selection at sea. Popular with families during the day, the atmosphere turns festive at night, especially during Rita's Fiesta, a fun evening of entertainment, dancing, drinks and a three-course dinner shared with friends old and new.

Rita's Cantina

Roasted Tomato-Tomatillo Broth

SOUP

1 1.5 pound (700 g) whole chicken,
well washed with cold water

5 cups (1.2 L) chicken broth (page 156)

2 bay leaves

1 fresh green chile, seeded and chopped

3 tablespoons (45 g) Achiote
paste, purchased

1 28-ounce (700 g) can tomatillos,
drained and chopped

1 large yellow onion, peeled and chopped

3 cloves garlic, peeled

4 large tomatoes, washed

2 tablespoons (30 ml) extra virgin olive oil

TORTILLAS

1/2 cup (120 ml) vegetable oil for frying

3 corn tortillas cut into thin strips

GARNISH

1/2 red bell pepper, julienned

1/2 yellow bell pepper, julienned

Cilantro sprigs

1 avocado, peeled, halved and
cut into small cubes

EQUIPMENT

Baking dish

Blender

Chef's knives and cutting board

Ladle

Paper towels

Shallow frying pan

Slotted ladle

Slotted spoon

Stockpot

Preheat oven to 350°F or 176°C.

Place chicken and broth in a large stockpot and bring
to a boil over medium-high heat. Add bay leaves, fresh
chile, Achiote paste and chopped tomatillos and mix well.
Reduce heat and simmer for 40 minutes or until chicken is
falling off the bone.

While chicken simmers, place chopped onions, garlic
and tomatoes in a baking dish. Drizzle with olive oil and
roast in the oven for 15 to 20 minutes or until the skin of
the tomatoes begins to blacken slightly. Remove from the
oven and peel tomatoes. Transfer tomatoes, roasted onions
and garlic to a blender. Process until smooth and add to
simmering soup.

Heat vegetable oil in a frying pan over medium-high
heat. Fry tortilla strips for 2 to 3 minutes or until golden
brown. Remove tortilla strips from hot oil using a slotted
spoon and drain on a plate lined with paper towels.

Ladle soup into warmed bowls, placing a mound of
shredded chicken in the center. Top with julienned
peppers and cilantro sprigs. Garnish with cubed avocado
and julienned tortillas.

Serves 6.

Difficulty 2.

Crackling Shrimp and Zucchini Chalupa

SALSA

3 ripe tomatoes, seeded, peeled and minced
2 ripe tomatoes, seeded, peeled and blended
2 cloves garlic, peeled and minced
2 jalapeño peppers, seeded and minced
1/2 red bell pepper, small diced
1/2 red onion, diced
1/4 bunch cilantro, minced
1 tablespoon (15 ml) extra virgin olive oil
Juice of 1/2 freshly squeezed lime
Salt and freshly ground black pepper

SALSA VERDE

1 12-ounce (340 g) can tomatillos, drained and chopped
3 jalapeños, seeded and minced
2 cloves garlic, peeled and minced
1/2 yellow onion, peeled and minced
1/2 cup (60 ml) chicken stock (page 156)
1/8 bunch fresh cilantro, chopped
Juice of 1 freshly squeezed lime
Salt to taste

TORTILLA BASKETS

6 soft garden spinach tortillas cut down (if needed) to 7 to 9-inches (17 to 22 cm) in diameter
1 cup (240 ml) vegetable oil

TEMPURA

1/2 cup (115 g) tempura flour
1/4 cup (60 ml) ice cold water
2 pounds (900 g) medium-sized shrimp (31-40 count), raw, peeled, deveined, tail off
2 zucchini cut in half, then into 1/4-inch (1 cm) thick slices

GARNISH

1/2 head of iceberg lettuce, shredded
1/2 red bell pepper, sliced with a vegetable peeler and kept in ice water
1/2 green bell pepper, sliced with a vegetable peeler and kept in ice water
1/2 yellow bell pepper, sliced with a vegetable peeler and kept in ice water
Guacamole (page 36)
Cilantro sprigs

EQUIPMENT

2 glass bowls
2.5-inch (6.3 cm) diameter cookie cutter
Blender
Chef's knives and cutting board
Deep saucepan
Metal tongs
Paper towels
Saucepan
Vegetable peeler

Mix all the ingredients for the salsa in a small glass bowl. Cover and refrigerate for 1 hour.

To make the salsa verde, place tomatillos, jalapeños, garlic, onions and chicken stock in a saucepan and bring to a boil over medium heat. Transfer to a blender and process to a coarse purée.

Pour mixture into a glass bowl and stir in cilantro and lime juice. Season with salt to taste. Cover and refrigerate for 3 hours.

To make tortilla baskets, warm vegetable oil in a deep pan over medium-high heat until it has reached a temperature of 350°F or 176°C.

Place metal tongs inside a cookie cutter. Dip a tortilla into hot oil and submerge it by positioning the tong-cookie cutter in the center of the tortilla and pressing down. The edges of the tortilla will lift up and around the cookie cutter, creating a basket form. Keep pressing for 2 minutes or until tortilla stops bubbling. Remove cookie cutter and use tongs to place the fried tortilla on a plate lined with paper towels to drain off the excess oil. Repeat with the other tortillas.

Place tempura flour in a glass bowl and whisk in water. Do not over-mix.

Using the same frying oil, dip shrimp and zucchini slices into the tempura batter and deep-fry for 2 to 3 minutes, turning often with metal tongs, until the batter is a light golden color. Remove shrimp and zucchini from oil and place on a plate lined with paper towels to drain the excess oil.

Place shredded lettuce inside the chalupa. Top with shrimp and zucchini tempura and strips of bell peppers. Garnish with cilantro sprigs. Serve with side dishes of salsa, salsa verde, sour cream and guacamole.

Serves 6.

Difficulty 2.

Champagne Margarita

1/2 oz. (1.5 cl) Patrón Silver Tequila
1/2 oz. (1.5 cl) Cointreau orange liqueur
1/2 oz. (1.5 cl) orange juice
Domaine Chandon, Brut, "Classic", California

Fill shaker with ice. Add all ingredients. Shake well, strain into a sugar-rimmed martini glass, fill with Domaine Chandon and garnish with a lime wedge.

Fajitas

MEATS

1 1/2 pounds (700 g) boneless,
skinless chicken breast sliced into strips
1 1/2 pounds (700 g) flank steak,
fat trimmed and sliced into strips
2 tablespoons (30 ml) extra virgin olive oil

MARINADE

Juice of 4 freshly squeezed limes
3 tablespoons (45 ml) extra virgin oive oil
1 teaspoon (5 g) dried oregano
1 clove garlic, peeled and chopped
1 jalapeño, seeded and chopped
1/4 bunch fresh cilantro chopped
1/2 teaspoon (2.5 g) ground cumin
1/4 teaspoon (1 g) ground chili
1 cup (240 ml) chicken stock (page 156)
Kosher salt

GUACAMOLE

2 large ripe avocadoes, halved, pit removed
Juice of 1 freshly squeezed lime
1/2 red onion, peeled and minced
1 Serrano chile, seeded and minced
1/4 bunch fresh cilantro, finely chopped
Salt and freshly ground black pepper
1 ripe tomato, seeded, peeled and chopped

PICO DE GALLO

3 large ripe tomatoes, seeded, peeled and diced
1 medium red onion, peeled and diced
1/4 bunch fresh cilantro, finely chopped
2 cloves garlic, peeled and minced
2 jalapeños, seeded and minced
Juice of 1 freshly squeezed lemon
Salt to taste

FAJITAS

2 tablespoons (30 ml) extra virgin olive oil
1 yellow onion, peeled and cut into strips
1 red onion, peeled and cut into strips
1 red bell pepper, seeded and cut into strips
1 green bell pepper, seeded and cut into strips
Salt
12 flour tortillas, purchased

GARNISH

2 green onions, chopped
1/8 bunch cilantro, chopped
Sour cream

EQUIPMENT

2 large bowls
2 small glass bowls
Blender
Carving knife
Cast iron fajita skillet
Chef's knives and cutting board
Large sauté pan
Plastic wrap
Potato ricer
Soup spoon

Meat must be marinated for 12 hours before you plan to serve the fajitas. Put chicken breast and flank steak into two separate bowls. Make marinade by putting all the ingredients in a blender and blend until smooth. Pour half of the marinade over the chicken and half over the flank steak and stir well. Cover and refrigerate overnight.

Preheat oven to 450°F or 230°C.

For guacamole, use a soup spoon to scoop out the avocado flesh and place in a small glass bowl. Sprinkle with lime juice to prevent discoloration and mash with a potato ricer.

Add onions, chile and fresh cilantro and mix well. Season with salt and pepper. Mix in tomatoes. Cover and refrigerate for 1 hour.

To make pico de gallo, place all the ingredients in a glass bowl and mix well. Cover and refrigerate for one hour.

Warm a cast iron fajita skillet in the oven for 10 to 12 minutes. Handle with care when removing from the oven.

For vegetables, warm oil in a large sauté pan over medium-high heat and sauté onions for 3 minutes or until onion is caramelized. Adjust heat to high. Add peppers to the onions and sauté for about 4 minutes or until peppers are slightly charred. Season with salt to taste. Transfer vegetables onto a platter and keep warm.

Drain the marinade from chicken and beef. Using the same sauté pan, warm olive oil over medium heat and sauté chicken and flank steak for 5 to 6 minutes or until thoroughly cooked, stirring continuously. Remove pan from heat and set aside for a couple minutes.

Mix sautéed chicken and flank steak with vegetables and arrange on the hot cast iron skillet. Garnish with chopped green onions and cilantro.

Serve immediately while still sizzling, accompanied by warm flour tortillas and side dishes of guacamole, sour cream and pico de gallo.

Serves 6.

Difficulty 2.

Rita's Cantina

Stuffed Ancho Chile Peppers

CHILI CON CARNE FILLING

2 tablespoons (30 ml) vegetable oil
1 yellow onion, peeled and chopped
1 clove garlic, peeled and crushed
1/2 green bell pepper, seeded and chopped
1 1/2 pounds (700 g) lean ground beef
1 tablespoon (15 g) tomato paste
1 16-ounce (455 g) can whole tomatoes,
    juice drained then chopped
1 teaspoon (5 g) paprika
2 teaspoons (10 g) chili powder
1/2 teaspoon (2.5 g) cayenne pepper
1 teaspoon (5 ml) Tabasco™
1 teaspoon (5 g) dried oregano
1 teaspoon (5 g) dried parsley
1/2 cup (120 ml) beef stock (page 157)
1 15-ounce (425 g) can kidney beans,
    drained and rinsed
Salt and freshly ground black pepper
1 pear, peeled, cored and diced small
1/3 cup (85 g) golden raisins, chopped
2 Roma tomatoes, seeded and diced small
1 cup (235 g) shredded jalapeño cheese mix

RICE

2 tablespoons (30 ml) canola oil
1 cup (235 g) long-grain Mexican white rice
1 cup (235 g) crushed tomato
1 tablespoon (15 g) Achiote paste
1 teaspoon (5 g) cumin powder
3 cups (720 ml) chicken stock (page 156)
1 dried chipotle pepper, soaked in water
1 teaspoon salt

PEPPERS

1 cup (240 ml) vegetable oil
12 large Anaheim chile or Ancho chile peppers
1 cup (230 g) all-purpose flour
1 tablespoon (15 g) cornstarch
1/2 teaspoon (2.5 g) baking powder
1/4 cup (60 ml) soda water
Pinch of salt

ALMOND CREAM

1/2 cup (120 ml) heavy cream
1 teaspoon (5 ml) almond extract
1/4 cup (60 ml) sour cream

VEGETABLES

1 tablespoon (15 ml) extra virgin olive oil
1 red onion, peeled and sliced
1/2 red bell pepper, sliced lengthwise
1/2 green bell pepper, sliced lengthwise
1/2 yellow bell pepper, sliced lengthwise
1/2 jalapeño, seeded and minced
Salt

GARNISH

1 cup (240 ml) salsa verde (page 35) mixed
    with 2 tablespoons (30 ml) heavy cream
Cilantro sprigs
Chopped cilantro

EQUIPMENT

2 glass bowls
2 large sauté pans
Carving knife, Chef's knives
    and cutting board
Deep frying pan
Metal tongs
Paper towels
Sauté pan
Slotted spoon
Small spoon
Wooden spoon

To make chili, warm oil in a large sauté pan over medium heat. Add onion and garlic and sauté for 3 minutes or until onion is translucent. Add peppers and ground beef and cook for 5 to 6 minutes or until beef is cooked throughout. Stir often with a wooden spoon. Incorporate tomato paste and chopped tomatoes. Season with spices and mix well. Stir in beef stock, mix well and bring to a boil. Reduce heat and simmer for 30 minutes, stirring occasionally.

Incorporate beans and cook, covered, for an additional 15 minutes.

Season with salt and pepper to taste and set aside half of the chili for future use.

Place the other half of the chili con carne in a large glass bowl. Add pears, raisins, diced tomatoes and shredded cheese and mix well.

For rice, warm oil in a large sauté pan over medium heat. Add rice and cook for about 5 minutes or until rice is well coated with oil and becomes a golden brown color. Add tomatoes. Season with spices and stir until well mixed. Add chicken stock and chipotle pepper and bring to a boil. Turn heat to low, cover and simmer rice for 20 minutes or until rice is cooked through and soft.

Remove rice from burner. Discard chipotle pepper. Season with salt to taste and fluff rice with a fork.

Place oil in a deep frying pan and warm over medium-high heat. Gently drop Anaheim or Ancho peppers into the hot oil and fry for 2 to 3 minutes or until skins start to blister. Remove from oil using metal tongs and place on a platter lined with paper towels to absorb excess oil. Set pan with oil aside. Let peppers cool for 10 minutes.

Carefully peel skin from cooled peppers, making sure not to tear the flesh.

Make a small incision on the side of the pepper or use an existing tear if there is one and insert a small spoon into the inside of the pepper. Gently scrape out the seeds and white membrane.

Spoon chili filling into peppers without forcing it. Do not over-stuff.

Prepare batter by mixing 1/2 cup (115 g) of flour, cornstarch, baking powder, soda water and salt together in a medium-sized glass bowl.

Roll stuffed peppers in the other 1/2 cup (115 g) of flour and dip in batter. Deep-fry the stuffed peppers in the frying pan for 3 minutes or until batter turns a golden brown color. Remove peppers from oil using a slotted spoon and place on platter lined with paper towels.

To make almond sauce, place heavy cream in a small saucepan and warm over medium heat. Add almond extract and whisk in sour cream. Remove from heat.

For vegetables, warm oil in sauté pan over medium heat and cook onions, peppers and jalapeño for 5 minutes or until vegetables are soft. Season with salt to taste.

Arrange rice on a warmed plate and top with a stuffed pepper. Drizzle with almond sauce and creamed salsa verde. Garnish with sautéed vegetables and fresh cilantro.

Serves 6.

Difficulty 4.

Rita's Cantina

Churros

CHOCOLATE SAUCES
3 cups (720 ml) heavy cream
1/2 cup (115 g) dark chocolate chips
1/2 cup (115 g) white chocolate chips
1/2 cup (115 g) milk chocolate chips

CHURROS
1 cup (235 g) all-purpose flour, sifted
1/3 teaspoon (1.5 g) baking powder
1 1/2 cups (360 ml) water
3 tablespoons (45 ml) vegetable oil
2 tablespoons (30 g) light brown sugar
1/2 teaspoon (2.5 g) salt

Vegetable oil for deep-frying

CINNAMON SUGAR
1/2 cup (115 g) granulated sugar
1 tablespoon (15 g) ground cinnamon
1 cinnamon stick, broken into pieces

EQUIPMENT
3 small saucepans
Deep dish
Deep fryer or deep frying pan
Glass bowl
Handheld mixer
Large star piping tip
Medium saucepan
Metal tongs
Paper towels
Paring knife
Piping or pastry bag

For chocolate sauces, divide heavy cream into 3 small saucepans and add a different type of chocolate chips to each pan. Bring to a simmer over low heat and cook until chocolates have melted, stirring often. Remove from heat and pour into individual serving containers.

To make churros, place flour and baking powder in a glass bowl and set aside.

Place water, oil, sugar and salt in a saucepan and bring to a boil over medium-high heat. Remove from heat and beat in flour mixture at low speed using a handheld electric mixer. Continue beating until the mixture forms a ball and leaves the sides of the pan clean.

Pour vegetable oil into a deep fryer or deep frying pan and warm over medium to high heat to a temperature of 375°F or 190°C.

Spoon churro batter into a pastry or piping bag or large plastic freezer bag fitted with a large star tip. Pipe mixture directly into hot oil in batches of four, using a knife to cut off pieces that are approximately 4 inches (10 cm) long as the batter emerges from the piping tip.

Deep-fry churros for 3 to 4 minutes or until golden brown, turning them often with metal tongs. Remove churros from hot oil and place on a plate covered with paper towels to drain the excess oil.

Mix sugar and cinnamon in a deep dish and roll churros in sugar mixture while still hot.

Serve churros on a platter with dishes of chocolate sauces.

Serves 6.

Difficulty 2.

Rita's Cantina

The Chef's Table is the ultimate destination for luxury dining onboard select ships in the Royal Caribbean International® fleet, an exclusive dinner for just 12 to 16 guests each night. The Executive Chef prepares and personally presents an elegant menu of five courses, each paired with a fine wine that complements and enhances the flavors. With exceptional cuisine, attentive service and an intimate atmosphere, Chef's Table offers guests a unique and informative gourmet experience in an exclusive setting.

Chef's Table

Spinach and Ricotta Blini

GRAVLAX
1 pound (480 g) salmon fillet
1 tablespoon (15 g) Kosher salt
2 tablespoons (30 g) granulated sugar
2 tablespoons (30 g) freshly ground pepper
1 tablespoon (15 g) fennel seeds,
lightly crushed
1 lemon, washed and sliced
1 bunch Fresh dill, chopped

ARTICHOKES
6 artichoke hearts, thawed and halved
1 clove garlic, peeled and chopped
1 tablespoon (15 ml) extra virgin olive oil

BLINIS
3/4 cup (175 g) all-purpose flour, sifted
1/2 teaspoon (2.5 g) baking soda
2 teaspoons (10 g) baking powder
3 eggs
1 3/4 cups (420 ml) buttermilk
Salt and freshly ground black pepper
3/4 cup (175 g) baby spinach, blanched, drained
and chopped
2 tablespoons (30 g) chopped parsley
2 tablespoons (30 g) chopped chives
2 green onions, finely chopped
3/4 cup (175 g) ricotta cheese
3 egg whites

SOUR CREAM
1/4 cup (60 g) sour cream
1 tablespoon (15 ml) vodka

LEMON VINAIGRETTE
Juice of 1 freshly squeezed lemon
1/4 cup (60 ml) extra virgin olive oil
Salt and freshly ground black pepper

VEGETABLES
2 seedless English cucumbers,
peeled and thinly sliced
4 red radishes, washed, thinly sliced
and placed in cold water
2 small red onions, peeled, thinly sliced
and placed in cold water
2 Belgian endives, washed, trimmed,
leaves cut in half lengthwise
Celery leaves

GARNISH
1 tablespoon (15 g) paddle fish caviar

EQUIPMENT
3 large glass bowls
4 small bowls
Baking dish
Chef's knives and cutting board
Electric mixer or handheld mixer
Griddle or non-stick frying pan
Paper towels
Piping bag
Plastic wrap
Small ladle
Small round cookie cutter
Small round piping tip
Small sauté pan
Tweezers
Whisk
Wooden spoon

Gravlax must be prepared at least 48 hours before you plan to serve the blini. Use tweezers to remove as many bones as possible from the salmon filet. Place filet on large piece of plastic wrap. Mix salt, sugar, pepper and fennel in a small bowl. Hand press mixture into exposed salmon flesh.

Top with lemon slices and dill and wrap tightly. Wrap in a second piece of plastic wrap. Place in a baking dish and refrigerate for 2 days.

Once cured (3 days maximum, as flavors intensify quickly), unwrap salmon. Discard lemon slices, dill and as much as possible of the salt mixture. Gently rinse under cold running water until all the salt is gone. Pat salmon dry with paper towels.

Place salmon on a cutting board and use a sharp knife to cut on the bias, starting with the tail end. All slices should be completely detached from the skin and placed on a platter.

Sauté artichokes and garlic in hot oil in a small sauté pan over medium-high heat. Transfer to a small dish. Cover and refrigerate for 2 hours.

To make blinis, place flour, baking soda, and baking powder in a large glass bowl and mix.

In a separate bowl, combine eggs, buttermilk, salt and pepper to taste and whisk until well mixed. Add wet ingredients to flour ingredients and whisk until smooth. Mix in spinach, freshly chopped herbs and ricotta cheese using a wooden spoon.

Place egg whites and a pinch of salt in a mixing bowl and beat with an electric mixer or handheld mixer set on medium speed until they forms soft peaks.

Fold egg whites into spinach batter with a wooden spoon.

Heat a griddle or non-stick frying pan on medium heat. Grease griddle with an oiled paper towel. Pour one ladleful of batter onto griddle to create 1-inch (2.5 cm) diameter pancakes.

When the surface of the pancakes start to bubble, flip over and cook the other side. Transfer pancakes to a platter and keep covered with a moistened paper towel so they don't dry out.

Mix sour cream and vodka in a small bowl. Spoon into a piping bag fitted with a small round tip.

Make vinaigrette dressing by mixing all ingredients together in a small glass bowl. Season with salt and pepper to taste.

Trim blinis to a uniform size and shape using a round cookie cutter.

Chill six entrée plates in the refrigerator. Place 3 blinis on each plate and add a dollop of sour cream. Carefully layer with vegetable slices, with artichokes at the bottom, followed by cucumbers then radishes. Drizzle with lemon vinaigrette and crown each assembled blini with a slice of gravlax, two red onion rings, an endive leaf and a celery leaf. Draw a line of sour cream on each plate and decorate with small dollops of paddle fish caviar.

Serves 6.

Difficulty 3.

WINE PAIRING ∽ MICHEL REDDE, SANCERRE, "LES TUILIÈRES", FRANCE

Chef's Table

Soup Trio (pages 46-49)

Sunchoke Soup

SOUP
1 tablespoon (15 g) unsalted butter
2 yellow onions, diced
3 stalks celery, diced
1 pound (450 g) sunchokes
(Jerusalem artichokes), peeled and sliced
1 clove garlic, peeled and minced
1 shallot, minced
1/4 cup (60 ml) dry white wine
2 cups (480 ml) chicken stock (page 156)
1 cup (240 ml) heavy cream
Salt and freshly ground white pepper

FROTH
1 cup (240 ml) 2% milk
5 peppercorns, cracked
3 sprigs thyme
1 cup (235 g) grated Parmigiano-Reggiano
2 teaspoons (10 g) salt

GARNISH
Thyme sprigs

EQUIPMENT
Chef's knife and cutting board
Food processor or blender
Heavy pots or stockpot
Large glass or stainless steel bowl
Large saucepan
Small saucepan
Small sauté pan
Wire whisk
Wooden spoon

In a heavy bottomed stockpot over medium heat, melt butter, then sauté onions and celery for 3 minutes or until onion is translucent. Add sunchokes, garlic and shallots and cook for 2 minutes. Deglaze with white wine and add chicken stock. Bring to a boil and simmer for 25 to 30 minutes or until sunchokes are tender to the touch. Transfer to a food processor and blend until smooth.

Pour mixture into a clean pot, whisk in heavy cream and bring to a simmer. Adjust seasoning with salt and pepper. Remove from heat and keep warm.

For froth, combine 1/4 cup (60 ml) milk, peppercorns and thyme in a small saucepan over medium heat and cook until milk bubbles around the edges.

Whisk in cheese and season with salt. Transfer to a glass bowl and let cool.

Finish froth just before serving, by placing a small amount of cheese mixture and milk in a small sauté pan over high heat. Whisk briskly until warm and frothy. Repeat as many times as necessary to get enough froth to garnish all the soup bowls.

To serve, pour soup into warmed soup bowls and garnish with a spoonful of froth and a sprig of thyme.

Serves 6.

Difficulty 3.

Asparagus Consommé

CONSOMMÉ
1 pound (450 g) asparagus spears, tips removed and set aside for later use
4 cups (960 ml) vegetable stock (page 156)
Salt and freshly ground black pepper
1/2 red bell pepper, cubed

EQUIPMENT
2 stockpots
Chef's knife and cutting board
Ladle
Mesh colander or cheesecloth

Place asparagus spears and vegetable stock in a stockpot and bring to a boil over high heat. Reduce heat and simmer for 1 hour. Strain through a cheesecloth or mesh colander into a clean pot and keep warm.

Bring to a boil just before serving. Add asparagus tips and cubed red peppers and cook for 2 minutes.

Ladle into warmed soup bowls and serve.

Serves 6.

Difficulty 1.

Tomato Bisque

BISQUE
6 Roma tomatoes, halved
1/4 cup (60 ml) extra virgin olive oil
Salt and freshly ground black pepper

1 medium yellow onion, peeled and
chopped
2 cloves garlic, peeled and chopped
1 tablespoon (15 ml) extra virgin olive oil
2 tablespoons (30 ml) dry white wine
2 cups (480 ml) tomato juice
1 bay leaf
1 thyme sprig
1/4 cup (60 ml) heavy cream
1 tablespoon (15 g) salted butter
Salt and freshly ground black pepper

BASIL CREAM
1/4 cup (60 ml) milk
1 bunch fresh basil, leaves only
1/4 cup (60 ml) whipping cream

EQUIPMENT
2 medium pots
Baking sheet
Blender
Chef's knife and cutting board
Food processor
Handheld mixer
Ladle
Parchment paper
Small glass bowl
Small saucepan
Whisk

Preheat oven to 350°F or 176°C.

Lay tomatoes face down on a baking sheet lined with parchment paper. Drizzle with olive oil and season with salt and pepper. Place in the oven and bake for 7 minutes. Remove tomatoes from the oven, let cool, then peel.

Sauté onion and garlic in hot oil in a medium-sized pot over medium-high heat. Add tomatoes. Deglaze with white wine. Add tomato juice, bay leaf and thyme sprig and bring to a boil. Season with salt and pepper. Reduce heat and simmer for 20 minutes.

Remove pot from heat. Discard bay leaf and thyme sprig. Transfer to a food processor and blend until smooth.

Pour soup into a clean pot. Whisk in heavy cream and butter a little at a time. Keep warm.

To make basil cream, place milk and basil leaves in a small saucepan and warm over medium heat. Simmer for 6 to 8 minutes or until liquid has reduced by half. Blend until smooth in a blender. Let cool.

Meanwhile, place whipping cream in a chilled glass bowl and beat at medium-high speed with a handheld mixer, until soft peaks form. Fold in basil mixture.

Ladle bisque in warmed soup bowls. Top with a small spoonful of basil cream and serve.

Serves 6.

Difficulty 2.

Elderflower Royale

1 1/2 oz. (4.5 cl) Elderflower liqueur
1/2 oz. (1.5 cl) lemon juice
Domaine Chandon, Brut, "Classic", California

Pour liqueur and lemon juice in a chilled champagne glass.
Fill with Domaine Chandon. Garnish with a lemon twist.

Miso-Brushed North Atlantic Black Cod

FISH
2 teaspoons (10 g) white miso paste
1 tablespoon (15 ml) mirin
(Japanese sweet cooking wine)
6 4-ounce (120 g) pieces of black cod
2 tablespoons (30 ml) vegetable oil

CANDIED LEMON PEELS
Reserved peels of 2 Meyer lemons, julienned
2 cups (480 ml) water
1 cup (235 g) sugar

PARSNIP PURÉE
4 parsnips, peeled and diced
2 large Idaho potatoes, peeled and quartered
1 tablespoon (15 g) sea salt

1 quart (900 ml) water
1 quart (900 ml) milk
1/4 cup (60 ml) heavy cream
2 tablespoons (30 g) butter
Salt and freshly ground white pepper

CARROT BEURRE BLANC
1 tablespoon (15 g) sugar
1 teaspoon (5 ml) water
2 Meyer lemons, peels reserved, lemons sliced
3 tablespoons (45 ml) dry white wine
4 carrots, juiced
1 carrot, peeled and sliced
1/3 cup (90 ml) fish stock (page 156)
2 tablespoons (30 ml) mirin
1/4 cup (60 ml) heavy cream

1/2 cup (115 g) chilled salted butter
Salt and freshly ground white pepper

BOK CHOI
1 tablespoon (15 ml) vegetable oil
1 clove garlic, peeled and minced
1/4 teaspoon (1.25 g) freshly grated ginger
10 pieces baby bok choi, trimmed
2 tablespoons (30 ml) water
Salt

GARNISH
1 ounce (60 g) micro greens

EQUIPMENT
Blender
Chef's knives and cutting board
Colander
Fine sieve
Food processor
Fork or small tongs
Large pot
Medium pot
Ovenproof dish
Plastic wrap
Platter
Saucepan
Sauté pan
Small glass bowl
Small mesh colander
Small saucepan
Whisk
Wire rack
Wok or shallow pan
Wooden spoon

Mix white miso paste and mirin in a small glass bowl.

Hand-rub onto the cod and transfer to a platter. Cover with plastic wrap and refrigerate for 2 hours.

To make candied lemon, add julienned lemon to a small saucepan filled with 1 cup (240 ml) of simmering water. Cook for 15 minutes and drain using a small mesh colander.

Combine sugar and remaining water in a small saucepan and bring to a simmer over medium heat, stirring often. Add lemon peels and cook for about 40 minutes or until peels are translucent and tender. Using a fork or small tongs, remove peels from syrup and arrange on a wire rack placed inside a cookie sheet. Let cool completely.

For purée, place parsnips and potatoes in a pot filled with salted cold water and milk, bring to a boil and cook until vegetables are easily pierced with the tip of a knife, about 15 minutes. Drain using a colander and place into a food processor. Blend until smooth. Add in cream, butter, salt and pepper, and pulse a few times to incorporate. Transfer to a medium-sized pot, cover and keep warm.

Meanwhile, to prepare beurre blanc, melt sugar and water in a saucepan over medium heat. Add lemon slices and cook for 4 to 5 minutes or until lemon slices are translucent.

Deglaze with white wine. Add carrot juice, sliced carrot, fish stock and mirin and bring to a boil. Reduce heat to low and simmer for 10 minutes or until sauce has reduced by half.

Add cream and simmer for 5 minutes or until sauce coats the back of a wooden spoon. Do not boil. Blend and strain through a fine sieve into a clean saucepan. Whisk in cold butter a little at a time. Season with salt and pepper. Set aside and keep warm.

For bok choi, warm oil in a wok or shallow pan over medium heat. Add garlic and ginger and sauté for 30 seconds. Add baby bok choi and toss to coat. Add water and season with salt. Cover and cook for 2 minutes.

Preheat the oven to 320°F or 160°C.

Heat oil in a large sauté pan over medium-high heat and sear cod for 2 minutes on each side. Transfer into an ovenproof dish and bake for 5 minutes.

Gently fold a few leaves of baby bok choi and place in the center of a warm plate. Top with cod.

Place several spoonfuls of parsnip purée on the plate. Drag the spoon through the purée in a left to right movement to create large tear-drop shapes.

Use the same technique to create tear-drop shapes with the carrot beurre blanc.

Garnish fish with candied Meyer lemon julienne and micro greens.

Serves 6.

Difficulty 3.

WINE PAIRING ❦ CHALK HILL, SAUVIGNON BLANC, SONOMA, CALIFORNIA

Chef's Table

WINE PAIRING ∽ CRAGGY RANGE, MERITAGE, "TE KAHU GIMBLETT GRAVELS VINEYARD", HAWKES BAY, NEW ZEALAND

Pink Roasted Beef Tenderloin with Black Truffle Spaetzle

TENDERLOIN

2 pounds (900 g) beef tenderloin, cleaned of fat and veins
Kosher salt and freshly ground black pepper
2 tablespoons (30 ml) vegetable oil

SPAETZLE (HOME-STYLE NOODLES)

1 ¹/2 cups (350 g) all-purpose flour
2 teaspoons (10 g) salt
3 eggs, lightly beaten
¹/3 cup (90 ml) milk
Freshly ground black pepper
2 tablespoons (30 g) salted butter
1 teaspoon (5 ml) black truffle oil
1 tablespoon (15 g) chopped parsley

PORT REDUCTION

¹/4 cup (60 ml) red wine
¹/4 cup (60 ml) port wine
1 cup (240 ml) demi-glace (page 157)

VEGETABLES

6 baby carrots, peeled, halved and blanched
12 green asparagus spears, peeled, trimmed and blanched
1 teaspoon (5 g) salted butter

GARNISH

Thyme sprigs

EQUIPMENT

Aluminum foil
Carving knife, Chef's knives and cutting board
Colander
Fine sieve
Large glass bowl
Large holed colander
Large pot
Large sauté pan
Ovenproof skillet
Sauté pan
Slotted spoon
Small pot
Small saucepan
Spatula
Whisk

Preheat oven to 400°F or 204°C.

Season beef tenderloin with salt and pepper on all sides. Warm oil in a large ovenproof skillet over medium-high heat. Add beef and sear on all sides until lightly browned.

Transfer to the oven and roast for about 25 minutes or until a thermometer inserted in the center of the roast reads 125°F or 52°C, for medium rare. Remove from oven. Tent loosely with aluminum foil and let rest for 10 to 15 minutes.

For spaetzle, mix all ingredients together in a large glass bowl until smooth. Let rest for 10 to 15 minutes.

Bring a pot of salted water to boil. Reduce heat to a simmer. To form spaetzle, hold a large holed colander above water and push about ¹/4 of the dough through the holes with a spatula. Cook for 3 to 4 minutes or until spaetzle float to the surface, stirring occasionally. Remove cooked spaetzle with a slotted spoon into a clean colander and rinse quickly with cool water. Repeat until all the dough has been used.

Transfer tenderloin to a carving surface or cutting board and slice crosswise into ¹/2-inch (1.2 cm) thick slices.

For sauce, place skillet on a stove burner set on high heat. Add red wine and port wine to the drippings in the pan and cook for 2 minutes, scraping the bottom of the pan. Add demi-glace and bring to a boil. Reduce heat and simmer for about 10 minutes or until liquid has reduced by half. Skim the surface of the liquid to remove excess fat. Pass liquid through a fine sieve into a small saucepan and set aside.

Melt butter in a large sauté pan over medium heat. Add spaetzle and sauté for 2 to 3 minutes or until warmed through. Drizzle with truffle oil and sprinkle with parsley. Keep warm.

Dunk carrots and asparagus in a small pot of boiling water then drain. Melt butter in a sauté pan over medium heat and sauté vegetables for 2 minutes.

To serve, arrange 2 slices of tenderloin in the center of warm plates. Place a spoonful of spaetzle on each side of the meat and top with carrots and asparagus spears. Drizzle with port reduction and garnish with thyme sprigs.

Serves 6.

Difficulty 2.

Orange Crunch Parfait

ORANGE CRUNCH PARFAIT	SABAYON	GARNISH	EQUIPMENT
½ teaspoon (2.5 ml) vegetable oil	*2 egg yolks*	*1 tablespoon (15 ml) ganache*	*2 glass bowls*
¼ cup (60 g) granulated sugar	*¼ cup (60 g) granulated sugar*	*Mint leaves*	*2 saucepans*
2 tablespoons (30 ml) water	*½ teaspoon (2.5 g) lemon zest*		*6 3-inch (7.6 cm) aluminum rings*
⅓ cup (85 g) slivered almonds, lightly toasted	*⅓ cup (85 g) mascarpone cheese*		*6 small ovenproof dessert dishes*
1 tablespoon (15 g) unsalted butter, melted	*4 ounces (120 g) fresh raspberries*		*Cookie sheet*
⅓ cup (90 ml) water	*4 ounces (120 g) fresh blueberries*		*Handheld mixer*
1 cup (240 g) granulated sugar	*3 ounces (85 g) fresh blackberries*		*Medium glass bowl*
½ cup (120 ml) orange liqueur			*Parchment paper*
Juice of 1 freshly squeezed orange			*Paring knife*
1 teaspoon (5 ml) orange extract			*Pastry brush*
Zest of 1 orange			*Small pastry torch (optional)*
12 egg yolks			*Spatula*
Zest of 1 lemon			*Wooden spoon*
3 ½ cups (840 ml) heavy cream			
2 tablespoons (30 ml) Grand Marnier			

Brush the sides of a small saucepan with vegetable oil. Add sugar and water and cook over high heat, stirring occasionally with a wooden spoon. Once sugar mixture is boiling, cover and cook for 3 minutes. Uncover and continue to cook the sugar until it turns a golden shade.

Remove from heat. Stir in almonds and pour mixture onto a cookie sheet lined with buttered parchment paper. Spread thin using a buttered spatula.

Let cool. Break off half of the caramelized almonds and chop. Break the other half into smaller pieces and set aside.

Bring water to a boil in a saucepan over high heat. Add sugar. Reduce heat and simmer for 10 minutes or until liquid has reduced by half. Add orange liqueur, orange juice and orange extract and simmer for another 5 minutes. Remove from heat and set aside.

Place egg yolks in a medium glass bowl and beat, at medium speed, with a handheld mixer. Add citrus zests. Drizzle in orange syrup, beating continuously until soft peaks form.

Place heavy cream in a chilled stainless steel or glass bowl. Using a handheld mixer, beat at medium speed until stiff peaks form. Fold in egg mixture a few spoonfuls at a time. Add chopped caramelized almonds and Grand Marnier and mix quickly.

Arrange aluminum rings on a cookie sheet lined with parchment paper. Fill each ring to the top with egg cream and freeze for 6 hours.

To make sabayon, place eggs, sugar and lemon zest in a glass bowl and place bowl inside a double boiler of simmering water. Beat mixture with a handheld mixer set at medium speed until it has doubled in volume and is creamy. Remove from heat and fold in mascarpone.

Preheat oven to broil.

Arrange ¾ of the berries in small ovenproof dishes. Top with a spoonful of sabayon and place on the top rack of your oven. Lightly brown sabayon, leaving the oven door open, or use a small pastry torch to brown the sabayon.

Dip a paring knife into hot water and run it along the inside of the aluminum rings to remove parfaits.

Arrange orange parfaits and sabayon on chilled dessert plates. Garnish parfait with remaining fresh berries and a mint leaf. Brush a little line of ganache on each plate and dust with small pieces of caramelized nuts.

Serves 6.

Difficulty 2.

Wine Pairing ⌘ Taittinger, Blanc de Blancs, Brut, Champagne, "Comtes de Champagne", France

Chef's Table

ROYAL CARIBBEAN INTRODUCED CHURRASCARIA-STYLE DINING WITH SAMBA GRILL, FEATURING AUTHENTIC BRAZILIAN AMBIANCE WITH LIVE MUSIC, COSTUMED DANCERS AND WAITSTAFF PREPARING CAIPIRINHAS, THE NATIONAL COCKTAIL OF CACHAÇA, LIME AND SUGAR, TABLESIDE. AND AS IN BRAZIL, GUESTS ENJOY A WIDE ARRAY OF APPETIZERS AND SALADS FROM AN EXPANSIVE BUFFET AND INDULGE IN THE DELICIOUS CHEESE ROLLS CALLED PAO DE QUEIJO. BUT MEAT IS THE MAIN ATTRACTION AT SAMBA GRILL. WAITERS BRING GIANT SKEWERS OF BEEF, LAMB AND PORK, PLUS SAUSAGES AND BACON-WRAPPED CHICKEN, ALL HOT OFF THE GRILL AND CARVED TO ORDER AT THE TABLE. AN ESSENTIAL EXPERIENCE FOR MEAT LOVERS.

Samba Grill

Appetizer Sampler (pages 58-61)

Marinated Green Lip Mussels

MUSSELS
1/4 cup (60 ml) water
2 pounds (900 g) green lip mussels
(about 15 mussels)

MARINADE
1 6-ounce (170 g) can crushed tomatoes
3 cloves garlic,
peeled and coarsely chopped
1/4 cup (60 ml) extra virgin olive oil
2 tablespoons (30 ml) red wine vinegar
1/2 teaspoon (2.5 g) salt
1/4 teaspoon (1 g) freshly
ground black pepper
1/8 bunch fresh cilantro, chopped

GARNISH
Chopped cilantro

EQUIPMENT
Blender
Chef's knives and cutting board
Large pot

Bring water to a boil in a large pot over high heat. Add mussels and steam for about 3 minutes or until mussels are open. Remove from heat and discard any mussels that have not opened. Allow to cool. Remove the top shell of each mussel and discard. Arrange the half mussels on a serving dish.

Place all the ingredients for the marinade in a blender and blend until smooth. Pour over mussels. Cover and refrigerate for 4 hours.

Sprinkle mussels with chopped cilantro just before serving.

Serves 6.

Difficulty 1.

Braised Fennel

FENNEL
1/2 teaspoon (2.5 g) caraway seeds
1 cup (240 ml) water
2 tablespoons (30 ml) freshly squeezed
orange or grapefruit juice
1/2 teaspoon (2.5 g) Kosher salt
4 fennel bulbs cut into wedges lengthwise
2 oranges or 1 pink grapefruit, peeled,
pith removed and sectioned
1/2 tablespoon (7.5 ml) white wine vinegar
1 teaspoon (5 ml) Tabasco™
2 teaspoons (10 ml) extra virgin olive oil
1 tablespoon finely chopped mint
1/2 teaspoon (2.5 ml) canola oil

GARNISH
Fennel sprigs

EQUIPMENT
Chef's knives and cutting board
Large glass bowl
Pastry brush
Saucepan

Warm grill to high heat.

Meanwhile, place caraway seeds, water, juice and salt in a saucepan and bring to a boil over medium-high heat. Reduce heat and simmer for 10 minutes.

Add fennel to pan and braise for 10 minutes.

Transfer fennel to a platter and remaining caraway stock to a glass bowl. Add vinegar, Tabasco™, olive oil and chopped mint to caraway stock.

Brush fennel with canola oil and place on the grill, leaving it just long enough to get marks on both sides.

Remove from grill and add to glass bowl, along with citrus sections. Gently toss with caraway stock. Refrigerate for 1 hour, then arrange on a serving platter. Garnish with fennel sprigs.

Serves 6.

Difficulty 2.

Caipirinha

1 1/2 limes, quartered
2 teaspoons (10 g) granulated sugar
2 oz. (6 cl) Leblon Cachaça

Muddle lime and sugar, add Cachaça, pour into a cocktail shaker filled with ice, shake well and roll into a double rocks glass.

Samba Grill

Sautéed Asparagus

ASPARAGUS
1 tablespoon (15 ml) extra virgin olive oil
1 bunch baby asparagus,
    peeled and trimmed
Salt and freshly ground black pepper

GARNISH
2 tablespoons (30 ml) balsamic vinegar
1/4 red bell pepper, finely diced
1/8 bunch fresh parsley, finely chopped

EQUIPMENT
Chef's knives and cutting board
Large sauté pan

Calamari And Broccoli Salad

SALAD
1 pound (450 g) broccoli florets, blanched
3 tablespoons (45 ml) extra
    virgin olive oil
1 large red onion, peeled and thinly sliced
1 clove garlic, peeled and sliced
1 red bell pepper, seeds removed and
    julienned
1 pound (450 g) squid body meat, cleaned,
    sliced into 1/2-inch rings
1/4 pound (125 g) squid tentacles, cleaned
1/4 teaspoon (2.5 g) chili flakes
Juice of 1 freshly squeezed lemon
Salt and freshly ground black pepper

GARNISH
1/8 bunch fresh parsley, chopped

EQUIPMENT
Chef's knives and cutting board
Large glass bowl
Large sauté pan

Grilled Radicchio With Balsamic Glaze

SALAD
4 radicchio heads, washed
    and cut into wedges
2 tablespoons (30 ml) extra virgin olive oil
2 oranges, peeled and sectioned

GLAZE
1/4 cup (60 ml) balsamic vinegar
1 tablespoon (15 ml) honey
Juice of 1 freshly squeezed lemon
Kosher salt and freshly
    ground black pepper

EQUIPMENT
2 glass bowls
Chef's knives and cutting board
Metal tongs
Paper towels
Pastry brush
Small saucepan
Whisk

Warm olive oil in a large sauté pan over medium-high heat. Add asparagus spears and sauté for 3 to 4 minutes, partially covered until tender, but still crisp. Season with salt and pepper.

Transfer to a serving platter. Drizzle with balsamic vinegar. Sprinkle with diced peppers and chopped parsley.

Serves 6.

Difficulty 1.

Place blanched broccoli florets in a large glass bowl.

Warm half of the olive oil in a large sauté pan over medium heat. Add onions, garlic and peppers and sauté for 5 minutes. Remove from heat and add to blanched broccoli.

Using the same pan, warm remaining olive oil over medium-high heat and sauté squid rings and tentacles for 3 minutes. Add chili flakes and deglaze with lemon juice. Remove from heat and add cooked squid to the vegetables. Season with salt and pepper to taste, then refrigerate for 1 hour.

Arrange on a serving platter and sprinkle with chopped parsley.

Serves 6.

Difficulty 1.

Warm grill to medium heat.

Pat radicchio wedges dry with a paper towel and brush with olive oil. Place on the grill and cook 2 minutes on each side, turning once. Remove from grill with tongs and arrange on a large platter with orange segments.

Meanwhile, pour vinegar in a small saucepan over medium heat and bring to a boil over high heat. Reduce heat and simmer for 6 to 8 minutes or until reduced to a syrupy consistency. Remove from heat. Whisk in honey and lemon juice.

Drizzle over radicchio and orange segments. Season with Kosher salt and pepper and serve lukewarm.

Serves 6.

Difficulty 1.

Mushrooms With Pesto

PESTO
8 to 10 bunches of basil leaves
3 cloves garlic, peeled
1/4 cup (60 g) pine nuts
1/3 cup (90 ml) extra virgin olive oil
Salt and freshly ground black pepper
1/4 cup (60 g) grated Pecorino cheese

SALAD DRESSING
2 tablespoons (30 ml) red wine vinegar
1 tablespoon (15 g) pesto
3 tablespoons (45 ml) extra virgin olive oil

MUSHROOMS
1/2 pound (250 g) button mushrooms,
quartered and blanched
1/2 pound (250 g) crimini mushrooms,
quartered and blanched

GARNISH
Fresh basil leaves
1 lemon, sliced very thin

EQUIPMENT
2 glass bowls
Chef's knives and cutting board
Food processor
Whisk

To make pesto, combine basil, garlic and pine nuts in a food processor and pulse until chopped. Add olive oil a little at a time and process until smooth. Season with salt and pepper. Transfer pesto to a glass bowl and mix in cheese. Cover and refrigerate.

For the salad dressing, place all the ingredients in a large glass or stainless steel bowl and whisk until blended. Toss in mushrooms. Cover and refrigerate for 1 hour.

Just before serving, mix mushrooms with pesto. Arrange in a chilled serving dish. Garnish with basil leaves and slices of lemon.

Serves 6.

Difficulty 1.

Seafood Salad

SALAD
2 tablespoons (30 ml)
extra virgin olive oil
1/2 pound (250 g) squid body meat,
cleaned, sliced into 1/2-inch rings
1/4 pound (125 g) squid tentacles, cleaned
1/4 pound (125 g) bay scallops
1/2 pound (250 g) medium-sized
cooked shrimp, peeled, deveined,
tail off and halved
1/2 red bell pepper, diced
1/2 green bell pepper, diced
1 medium red onion, peeled and diced
1/8 bunch parsley, finely chopped
Salt and freshly ground black pepper

SEMI DRIED TOMATOES
3 Roma tomatoes, halved
2 tablespoons (30 ml) extra virgin olive oil
Salt and freshly ground black pepper

GARNISH
Basil sprig

EQUIPMENT
2 glass bowls
Baking sheet
Chef's knives and cutting board
Large bowl
Large sauté pan
Parchment paper

Preheat oven to 260°F or 126°C.

Lay tomatoes face up on a baking sheet lined with parchment paper. Drizzle with olive oil and season with salt and pepper. Place in the oven and bake for 10 minutes or until tomatoes are semi dried (slightly shrunken but still soft).

Heat olive oil in a large sauté pan over medium heat. Sauté squid rings and tentacles, and bay scallops for 3 to 4 minutes. Transfer to a large glass bowl. Add remaining ingredients, including semi dried tomatoes, and mix well. Season with salt and pepper.

Arrange on a serving platter. Garnish with basil sprig.

Serves 6.

Difficulty 1.

Feijoada

MEAT

1 pound (450 g) carne seca, purchased in a Brazilian specialty shop

½ pound (250 g) salted slab of bacon

½ pound (250 g) linguiça sausage or sweet Italian pork sausage

1 pound (450 g) baby back spareribs

BEANS

2 pounds (900 g) dried black beans, washed, picked clean

1 tablespoon (15 ml) vegetable oil

1 medium yellow onion, peeled and chopped

2 cloves garlic, peeled and chopped

2 carrots, peeled and chopped

2 celery stalks, chopped

2 quarts (1.8 L) chicken stock (page 156)

2 bay leaves

Salt and freshly ground black pepper

RICE

2 tablespoons (30 ml) extra virgin olive oil

1 small yellow onion, peeled and chopped

1 clove garlic, peeled and chopped

1 whole clove

2 cups (465 g) long-grain white rice

5 cups (1.2 L) chicken stock (page 156)

KALE

1 tablespoon (15 ml) extra virgin olive oil

1 pound (450 g) kale, washed, dried, stems and middle membrane removed, leaves julienned

Salt and freshly ground black pepper

EQUIPMENT

2 large stockpots

Carving knife, Chef's knives and cutting board

Colander

Fork

Ladle

Large sauté pan

Medium saucepan

Metal tongs

Small stockpot

Wooden spoon

Place carne seca and salted pork in a large stockpot. Cover with cold water and refrigerate 6 hours, changing the water once.

Place the black beans in a second stockpot. Cover with cold water and soak for 6 hours.

Remove carne seca and salted pork from water. Discard water, wash the stockpot and return the meat to the pot. Cover with cold water and bring to a boil over high heat. Reduce heat to medium low and simmer for 10 minutes. Remove meats from liquid and place meats on a platter. Discard liquid.

Prick sausages with a fork and place in a small stockpot. Cover with cold water and bring to a boil. Reduce heat to low and simmer for 15 minutes. Remove sausages from the pot using metal tongs and set them aside on the same platter with the carne seca and salted bacon.

Split baby back ribs in two.

Drain the beans using a colander and rinse.

Warm oil in a large stockpot over medium heat and sauté onion and garlic for 2 minutes or until onion is translucent. Add carrots, celery and beans and cook for 2 minutes. Add carne seca, salted bacon, sausages and baby back ribs and sauté for 5 minutes, stirring often. Add chicken stock and bay leaves and simmer, partially covered, for 1 ½ hours, stirring occasionally. Season with salt and pepper to taste.

To prepare rice, heat oil in a medium saucepan over medium heat. Add onion, garlic and whole clove and sauté for 3 minutes or until onion is translucent. Add rice and cook for 3 to 4 minutes, stirring constantly until rice has absorbed all the oil and all the grains are coated. Stir in chicken stock and bring to a boil over high heat. Reduce heat and simmer, covered, for 20 minutes or until rice is tender. Remove from heat and let stand, covered, for 5 minutes to allow rice to absorb any remaining liquid.

To make kale, heat oil in a large sauté pan over medium heat. Add kale, season with salt and pepper to taste and toss. Cook for 2 to 3 minutes or until kale is wilted, but still slightly crisp and bright green in color.

Remove several ladlefuls of beans from the pot and mash them with a fork. Put back into the pot to thicken the stew.

Simmer over low heat for another 30 minutes or until beans are soft and the stew has a creamy consistency. Remove the bay leaves. Ladle bean stew into warmed individual bowls.

Remove the meats from the stew. Slice the carne seca and pork crosswise. Cut ribs and slice sausages into angled discs. Arrange on a large ceramic platter with Brazilian rice and wilted kale and serve family style.

Serves 6.

Difficulty 3.

Picanha

SALSA CRIOLLA
2 red bell peppers
2 Roma tomatoes, halved
4 cloves garlic, peeled
1/3 cup (90 ml) extra virgin olive oil
1/4 teaspoon (1.25 g) red pepper flakes
Kosher salt

CHIMICHURRI SAUCE
4 tomatillos, husk removed and halved
2 tablespoons (30 ml) extra virgin olive oil
Salt and freshly ground black pepper

5 cloves garlic, peeled and chopped
2 shallots, peeled and chopped
1/2 bunch fresh parsley,
stems removed and finely chopped

10 basil leaves, finely chopped
1/2 jalapeño, seeded and minced
1 tablespoon (15 g) dried oregano
1/2 teaspoon (2.5 g) salt
Juice of 2 freshly squeezed lemons
1 cup (240 ml) extra virgin olive oil

MARINADE
4 cloves garlic, peeled and chopped
1/4 cup (60 ml) extra virgin olive oil
1 tablespoon (15 g) rock salt

PICANHA
2 pounds (900 g) beef top sirloin cap roast
(Picanha cut), with fat cap left on

FAROFA
1/4 pound (125 g) bacon, diced small
1 tablespoon (15 ml) palm oil
1/2 cup (115 g) salted butter, room temperature
1 large yellow onion, finely chopped
1 clove garlic, peeled and minced
1/4 red bell pepper, diced
1/4 green bell pepper, diced
2 cups (465 g) manioc flour
Salt and freshly ground black pepper
1/4 cup (60 g) chopped black olives
1 hard-boiled egg, chopped
1/8 bunch of fresh parsley,
stems removed and finely chopped

EQUIPMENT
Baking sheet
Blender
Carving knife
Carving knife, Chef's knives
and cutting board
Glass bowl
Large sauté pan
Mortar
Ovenproof dish
Parchment paper
Plastic wrap
Rotisserie spit
Small glass bowl

Preheat oven to 300°F or 148°C.

For salsa criolla, place peppers, Roma tomatoes and garlic in an ovenproof dish. Drizzle with 2 tablespoons (30 ml) olive oil. Roast for 20 minutes. Place peppers into a small bowl and cover with plastic wrap or a small, tightly closed paper bag to loosen the skins and ease peeling. Set aside for 30 minutes.

Peel peppers and remove seeds. Place in a blender with roasted Roma tomatoes, garlic, red pepper flakes and half of the remaining oil. Blend for 30 seconds. With the motor running, slowly add remaining oil in. Season with Kosher salt and transfer to a serving dish. Cover and refrigerate.

To make the chimichurri sauce, lay the tomatillos face up on a baking sheet lined with parchment paper. Drizzle with olive oil and season with salt and pepper. Place in the oven and roast for 30 minutes or until tomatillos are soft.

Place tomatillos in a blender and process to a coarse purée. Transfer to a glass bowl and set aside.

Using the same blender, blend all the remaining ingredients together to a fine purée. Add to the tomatillo mixture and stir. Cover and refrigerate for at least 2 hours.

For the marinade, place all the ingredients in a mortar and crush into a paste.

Cut picanha into 3-inch (7.5 cm) thick steaks. Skewer meat onto a rotisserie spit, bending them into a C shape with the fat cap on top. Rub marinade and salt on the steaks and set aside on a platter for 30 minutes.

Set the grill up for rotisserie cooking at the highest temperature available (all burners on) and place the drip pan in the middle of the grill.

To make farofa, place bacon in a large sauté pan over medium heat and cook for 3 to 4 minutes or until crispy. Remove bacon from pan and set aside.

Discard 3/4 of the bacon fat from the pan. Add palm oil and butter to the pan and heat until butter melts. Add onion and garlic and sauté for 3 to 4 minutes or until onion is translucent. Add peppers and cook for 3 minutes.

Add manioc to the vegetables and cook for 4 to 5 minutes. Season with salt and pepper to taste and keep warm on the side of the stove. When ready to serve, warm over medium heat and stir in chopped olives, egg and parsley.

Place the spit on the rotisserie, and start the motor. Close the lid of the grill and reduce the temperature to medium high.

Cook the steaks until the internal temperature reaches 115°F (46°C) for rare or 125°F (52°C) for medium-rare or about 20 to 30 minutes.

Slice picanha at the table using a very sharp carving knife. Serve with farofa, salsa criolla and chimichurri sauce.

Serves 6.

Difficulty 2.

Caipiroska

1 1/2 limes, quartered
2 teaspoons (10 g) granulated sugar
2 oz. (6 cl) Stolichnaya® vodka

Muddle lime and sugar, add vodka, pour in to a cocktail shaker filled with ice, shake well and roll into a double rocks glass.

Samba Grill

Brigadeiro

SIMPLE SYRUP
1/4 cup (60 g) granulated sugar
1/3 cup (90 ml) water
2 tablespoons (30 ml) rum

PASTRY CREAM
2/3 cup (160 ml) whole milk
1 teaspoon (5 ml) vanilla extract
1/4 cup (60 g) granulated sugar
2 tablespoons (30 g) unsalted butter
1/4 cup (60 g) all-purpose flour
3 egg yolks
1/2 cup (120 ml) heavy cream

GÉNOISE
4 eggs
2/3 cup (140 g) sugar
3/4 cup (175 g) all-purpose flour, sifted
2 tablespoons (30 g) unsalted butter, melted
1/4 cup (60 g) cocoa powder, sifted

GANACHE
1/3 cup (85 g) dark chocolate
1 tablespoon (15 g) unsalted butter
1/3 cup (90 ml) heavy cream

GARNISH
Pint fresh raspberries
Pint fresh blackberries, halved

ACCENTS
Chocolate rings, twirls, fans, purchased

EQUIPMENT
2 large stainless steel or glass bowls
3-inch (7.6 cm) round cookie cutter
4 small saucepans
6 3-inch (7.6 cm) aluminum rings
Baking dish
Cookie sheet
Handheld mixer
Large round piping tip
Medium saucepan
Parchment paper
Paring knife
Pastry brush
Piping bag or plastic sandwich bag
Whisk
Wire rack

Preheat oven to 350°F or 180°C.

Prepare syrup by mixing sugar and water in a small saucepan and boiling until sugar has melted. Let cool, then add rum.

For pastry cream, combine milk, vanilla extract and sugar in a saucepan and bring to a boil. Remove from heat.

Over medium heat, melt butter in a medium-sized saucepan, then slowly whisk in flour. Pour in the hot milk a little at a time, whisking constantly. Cook over low heat until mixture begins to pull away from the sides of the saucepan, about 4 to 5 minutes. Do not boil.

Remove from heat and slowly fold in egg yolks, one at a time. Let cool and set aside.

Lay parchment paper on a cookie sheet. Grease and dust with flour.

To make génoise, place eggs in a large glass bowl set over a pan of hot water. Add sugar and whisk until mixture is thick, creamy and has doubled in volume. Fold in butter then flour and cocoa powder a little at a time.

Spread mixture on the parchment paper. Bake for 10 to 12 minutes or until a toothpick inserted in the génoise comes out clean.

Remove génoise from the oven and let cool on a wire rack for 30 minutes.

For the ganache, place chocolate, butter and cream in a small saucepan and warm over low heat, stirring often, until chocolate has melted. Remove from heat and set aside.

Cut génoise into 18 disks using a 3-inch (7.6 cm) round cookie cutter. Brush génoise disks with simple syrup.

Place heavy cream in a chilled stainless steel or glass bowl and, using a handheld mixer, beat at medium speed until stiff peaks form. Fold into cooled pastry cream. Add ganache to cream mixture and mix well. Spoon chocolate cream into a piping bag or plastic sandwich bag fitted with a large, open, smooth tip.

Place one layer of génoise disks into 6 3-inch aluminum rings or chocolate rings. Cover with chocolate cream. Repeat twice, finishing with a layer of chocolate cream. Refrigerate for 3 hours.

Place berries and remaining simple syrup in a small saucepan and warm over medium heat. Simmer for 5 minutes.

If using aluminum rings, run a thin knife on the inside of each ring to loosen the sides of the Brigadeiro and then lift the ring off. Arrange on chilled dessert plates. Garnish with chocolate accents and a couple spoonfuls of berry compote.

Serves 6.

Difficulty 4.

Antique woods and high-back settees, plush velvet, burnished copper and a wine bar for the ages, certainly for carefully aged fine wines.

Don't let the atmosphere distract you from the main attraction in Vintages. Our wonderful wines, tasty tapas and sample wine flights have been created to unite four of the world's most famous names in the history of wine — Robert Mondavi, Caymus, Beringer Blass and Niebaum Coppola.

A feature found nowhere else, Vintages holds the largest handcrafted wine bottle in the world. This one-of-a-kind item was donated by Caymus Vineyards and was designed to be the focal point of the bar.

This bottle holds 152 gallons (575 liters) of wine, has a height of 99.15 inches or 8.26 feet (2.52 meters), a circumference of 79¼ inches (2 meters) at the base and weighs 260 lbs (118 kg) empty and 1,528 pounds (693 kg) full.

Find a cozy corner and gather with friends for some mocha-inflected merlot and enticing platters of tapas. Savor the tantalizing combinations of tastes and textures and let our knowledgeable Wine Tenders lead the way.

Vintages

Croquetas de Pollo con Revuelto de Cebollinas
(Chicken Croquettes with Chive Rémoulade)

CHIVE RÉMOULADE
1 cup (240 ml) mayonnaise
1 tablespoon (15 ml) Worcestershire sauce
Juice of half lemon
1 teaspoon (5 ml) Tabasco™
1 medium yellow onion, diced
2 stalks celery, diced
1 clove garlic, peeled and minced
1/4 bunch fresh parsley, chopped
1/2 bunch chive, chopped
Salt and freshly ground black pepper

CROQUETAS
2 cups (480 ml) chicken stock (page 156)
2 chicken quarters, skin on
2 pounds (900 g) Yukon Gold potatoes, peeled and quartered
2 tablespoons (30 ml) olive oil
1 small onion, diced
2 cloves garlic, peeled and diced
1 egg yolk
Salt and freshly ground black pepper

CRUST
1/2 cup (115 g) all-purpose flour
1 egg, beaten
1 cup (235 g) breadcrumbs
2 cups (480 ml) canola oil for frying

EQUIPMENT
4 baking sheets
4 stockpots
Frying pan
Glass or stainless steel bowl
Paper towels
Parchment paper
Potato ricer
Small sauté pan
Spoon
Wooden spoon

Preheat oven to 200°F or 95°C.

To make rémoulade, mix all ingredients in a glass or stainless steel bowl. Season with salt and pepper, cover and refrigerate for 4 hours.

In a medium stockpot over medium-high heat, bring chicken stock to a boil. Add chicken quarters and simmer for 20 minutes or until cooked through. Allow to cool, remove skin, pull meat off the bone and dice.

Place potatoes into salted cold water, bring to a boil and cook until potatoes are easily pierced with the tip of a knife, about 15 minutes. Drain and transfer into a sheet pan.

Place in the oven for 10 minutes to allow moisture to evaporate.

Meanwhile, in a small sauté pan over medium heat, warm oil and sauté onion and garlic for 4 minutes or until onion is translucent. Do not brown.

Press potatoes through a potato ricer into a heated bowl. Add chicken, onion mixture and egg yolk. Season with salt and pepper and mix well. Spread mixture onto a baking sheet and let cool.

Using a spoon, divide mixture into 18 equally sized balls and roll in your hands to make small cylinders. Roll first into flour, then dip in egg and finally into the breadcrumbs. Set aside on a baking sheet lined with parchment paper.

In a small frying pan over medium-high heat, warm oil and deep-fry croquetas in batches, making sure they are completely submerged in hot oil, for 1 to 2 minutes or until golden. Transfer to a paper towel-lined tray and let drain. Season with salt and keep warm in the oven. Serve with rémoulade.

Serves 6.

Difficulty 2.

Tortilla de Patatas (Spanish Potato Omelet)

TORTILLA
5 large Idaho potatoes, peeled, thinly sliced and reserved in cold water
3 tablespoons (45 ml) extra virgin olive oil
3 white onions, peeled and thinly sliced
6 eggs, beaten
Salt and freshly ground black pepper

GARNISH
Paprika
Parsley sprigs

EQUIPMENT
Chef's knife and cutting board
Large frying pan
Non-stick, ovenproof baking dish
Paper towels
Sauté pan
Tray

Preheat oven to 350°F or 175°C.

For tortilla, blanch potatoes in hot oil. Drain and place on a paper towel-lined tray.

In a sauté pan over medium heat, warm oil and sauté onions for 10 to 15 minutes or until onions are caramelized. Season with salt and pepper.

Grease a non-stick, ovenproof baking dish and layer potatoes and onions alternately. Pour in egg batter and bake for 15 minutes.

Cut tortilla in wedges, sprinkle with paprika and garnish with parsley.

Serves 6.

Difficulty 1.

Setas a la Parrilla, Pimietos, Calabacín, y Espárragos (Grilled Mushrooms, Peppers, Zucchini and Asparagus Platter)

GARLIC CONFIT
1 head garlic, peeled and shaved
1/3 cup (90 ml) extra virgin olive oil

VEGETABLES
1/3 cup (90 ml) extra virgin olive oil
3 medium portabella mushrooms, thickly sliced
15 asparagus spears, blanched
1 eggplant, thickly sliced
2 zucchini, cut lengthwise
2 yellow squash, cut lengthwise
Salt and freshly ground white pepper
1 red bell pepper
1 green bell pepper

GARNISH
Chopped parsley

EQUIPMENT
Chef's knife and cutting board
Grill pan or outdoor grill
Metal tongs and spatula
Pastry brush
Small saucepan

To make garlic confit, in a small saucepan over medium heat, simmer garlic in olive oil for 20 minutes. Do not brown. Allow to cool. Cover and reserve.

To grill the vegetables:

Outdoor grill: Heat to medium-high. Lightly brush cut sides of vegetables with olive oil, season with salt and pepper and place on grill. Grill each set of vegetables for 3 to 5 minutes, turning only once. Remove from grill, transfer to a deep platter, and liberally brush with garlic confit, cover and refrigerate.

Indoor grill: Lightly oil a grill pan. Set temperature to medium-high heat. Brush cut sides of vegetables with olive oil, season with salt and pepper and place on grill. Grill each set of vegetables for 5 to 7 minutes, turning only once. Remove from grill, transfer to a deep platter, and liberally brush with garlic confit, cover and refrigerate.

Arrange vegetables on small chilled plates and sprinkle with chopped parsley.

Serves 6.

Difficulty 1.

Pan amb Tomaquet
(Tomato-rubbed Crostinis)

Sangria

TOASTS
1 sourdough bread, purchased and thickly sliced
3 tablespoons (45 ml) extra virgin olive oil
2 cloves garlic, peeled
6 ounces (170 g) cherry tomatoes, halved
Salt and freshly ground black pepper

EQUIPMENT
Baking sheet
Chef's knife and cutting board
Parchment paper
Pastry brush

1 bottle (75 cl) red wine
1/3 cup (90 ml) Cointreau or Grand Marnier
1/3 cup (90 ml) gin
1/3 cup (90 ml) dark rum
1/3 cup (90 ml) lemon or orange-flavored vodka
1 1/2 cups (360 ml) orange juice
1/2 cup (115 g) sugar
1 orange, washed and thinly sliced
2 lemons, washed and thinly sliced
1 apple, washed, cored and cubed
2 peaches, washed, pitted and cubed
1 1-liter bottle carbonated lemon-flavored soda

GARNISH
1 orange, sliced
2 limes, sliced

EQUIPMENT
Chef's knife and cutting board
Large glass or plastic serving pitcher

Preheat oven to 400°F or 204°C.

To make toast, lightly brush bread slices with olive oil, place on a baking sheet lined with greased parchment paper and bake for 2 to 3 minutes or until bread slices are golden.

Allow bread slices to cool and rub first with garlic then tomatoes.

Sprinkle with remaining olive oil and season with salt and pepper.

Arrange on a side plate and serve with remaining tomatoes drizzled with olive oil.

Serves 6.

Difficulty 1.

To make sangria, place all ingredients into a large pitcher with the exception of the carbonated lemon-flavored soda. Mix well and refrigerate overnight.

Stir in carbonated lemon-flavored soda just before serving.

Pour sangria into chilled glasses garnished with an orange and lime slice.

Serves 6.

Difficulty 1.

WINE PAIRING ⌒ PACO ET LOLA, ALBARIÑO, RIAS BAIXAS, SPAIN

Ensalada de Pulpo (Octopus Salad)

OCTOPUS
1 1/2 pounds (700 g) baby octopus or squid
1 large yellow onion, peeled and studded with 5 cloves
2 bay leaves

SALAD
1 small cauliflower, cut in small florets and blanched
1 medium yellow onion, peeled and diced
1 green bell pepper, diced
12 small caper berries
1/2 fennel bulb, trimmed and diced
2 cloves garlic, peeled and minced
1/4 cup (60 ml) sherry vinegar
Juice of 1 lemon
1/2 cup (120 ml) extra virgin olive oil
Sea salt and freshly ground black pepper

EQUIPMENT
Chef's knife and cutting board
Large glass or stainless steel bowl
Slotted spoon
Stockpot

For octopus, in a stockpot over high heat, bring salted water to a boil. Add the octopus, studded onion and bay leaves. Bring back to a boil and simmer for 15 minutes or until tender.

Using a slotted spoon, remove octopus from broth and let cool on a plate.

In a large glass or stainless steel bowl, mix together the salad ingredients. Add octopus and mix well. Season with salt and pepper. Cover and refrigerate for 2 hours.

Serves 6.

Difficulty 1.

Cippolline al Vinagre Balsamico (Balsamic Marinated Baby Onions)

1/4 cup (60 ml) extra virgin olive oil
1 tablespoon (15 g) unsalted butter
1 1/2 pounds (700 g) baby onion, peeled
2 tablespoons (30 g) granulated sugar
1 cup (240 ml) balsamic vinegar
1 rosemary sprig
1 cup (240 ml) water

GARNISH
Thyme sprigs

EQUIPMENT
Chef's knife and cutting board
Medium glass bowl
Medium sauté pan

In a sauté pan over medium heat, warm oil and butter. Add onions and sauté for 8 to 10 minutes or until onions are lightly brown on all sides.

Add sugar, vinegar, rosemary sprig and water and bring to a boil. Reduce heat and simmer, uncovered, for about 10 minutes or until onions are al dente.

Transfer onions to a glass bowl. Let cool, cover and refrigerate for 2 hours.

Serve in a small platter and garnish with thyme sprigs.

Serves 6.

Difficulty 2.

Pimientos Piquillo Rellones De Queso Feta, y Alcachofas a la Plancha, (Cheese-Stuffed Piquillo Peppers and Grilled Vegetables)

PIQUILLO PEPPERS
1/2 cup (115 g) cream cheese
1/3 cup (85 g) feta cheese, crumbled
2 tablespoons (30 g) freshly minced parsley or chives
Salt and freshly ground black pepper
1 7.5-ounce can (225 g) whole piquillo peppers, drained

GRILLED VEGETABLES
3 pieces baby artichokes, cleaned and halved
1 medium size eggplant, cut into thin slices
1/4 cup (60 ml) extra virgin olive oil
Salt and freshly ground black pepper

GARNISH
Caper berries
Fresh basil

EQUIPMENT
Baking pan
Chef's knife and cutting board
Grill pan or outdoor grill
Pastry brush
Small sauté pan

For piquillo peppers, in a small sauté pan over low heat, soften cream cheese. Remove from heat and incorporate feta cheese and fresh herbs. Season with salt and pepper and let cool.

Stuff piquillo peppers with cheese mixture and refrigerate.

Meanwhile, brush artichokes and eggplant slices with olive oil and season with salt and pepper.

Grease a grill pan and heat to medium high. Place vegetables in the pan, marking each side with grill marks.

Place eggplants into a small sheet pan, season with salt and pepper and drizzle with remaining olive oil. Cover and refrigerate.

Remove artichokes from grill and transfer into a small plate. Let cool.

Arrange cheese stuffed piquillo peppers and grilled vegetables on small dishes and garnish with caper berries and fresh basil.

Serves 6.

Difficulty 1.

Boquerones en Aceite de Oliva y Zumo de Limón (White Anchovies in Lemon Oil)

1 6-ounce can (170 g) marinated white anchovies, purchased
18 green olives stuffed with red peppers
Fresh parsley

Wrap olives with anchovies and arrange on a small plate. Cover and refrigerate.

Decorate with a parsley sprig at the last minute.

Serve tapas with an assortment of olives and a platter of thinly sliced Serrano ham.

Serves 6.

Difficulty 0.

Brocheta de Chorizo con Camarones y Vieiras

(Garlicky Seafood and Chorizo Skewers)

GARLIC CONFIT
1 head garlic, peeled and shaved
1/3 cup (90 ml) extra virgin olive oil

KEBABS
12 small wood skewers, soaked in warm water
12 sea scallops
3 spicy chorizo sausages,
cut diagonally in thick slices
12 large sized shrimp, peeled, deveined, tail on
1/4 cup (60 ml) extra virgin olive oil
Salt and freshly ground black pepper

GARNISH
Chopped parsley
1 small red onion, halved and lightly grilled
Parsley sprigs

EQUIPMENT
12 stainless steel skewers
Baking dish
Chef's knife and cutting board
Grill pan (if outdoor grill is not available)
Pastry brush
Small saucepan

In a small saucepan over medium heat, simmer garlic in olive oil for 20 minutes. Do not brown. Allow to cool. Cover and reserve.

Thread the sea scallops and chorizo sausage through their center on skewers. Repeat with the shrimp. Transfer kebabs into a baking dish, brush with garlic confit, drizzle with olive oil and season with salt and pepper. Cover and refrigerate for 2 hours.

To grill kebabs:

Outdoor grill: Heat to medium-high and place kebabs on grill. Cook each kebab for 3 to 5 minutes, turning only once. Remove from grill and transfer on a platter.

Indoor grill: Heat to medium-high and place kebabs on grill. Cook each kebab for 3 to 5 minutes, turning only once. Remove from grill and transfer on a platter.

Sprinkle kebabs with chopped parsley and garnish platter with a grilled onion and some parsley sprigs.

Serves 6.

Difficulty 1.

WINE PAIRING ☞ TORRES MILMANDA, CHARDONNAY, CONCA DE BARBERÀ, SPAIN

Vintages

Gazpacho

GAZPACHO
2 cups (480 ml) tomato juice
1/2 cup (120 ml) water
1/4 cup (60 ml) red wine vinegar
1/4 cup (60 ml) extra virgin olive oil
1 small red onion, chopped
2 cloves garlic, peeled and chopped
1/4 cup (60 g) breadcrumbs
1 teaspoon (5 g) ground cumin
1 teaspoon (5 g) celery salt
1 tablespoon (15 ml) Worcestershire sauce
Tabasco™ sauce, to taste

CROSTINIS
1 French baguette, sliced
2 tablespoons (30 ml) extra virgin olive oil

GARNISH
1 small red onion, diced
Parsley

EQUIPMENT
Baking sheet
Chef's knife and cutting board
Chinois or fine mesh sieve
Large glass or stainless steel bowl
Pastry brush

Preheat oven to 350°F or 175°C.

Mix all ingredients into a large glass bowl. Cover and refrigerate overnight.

For crostinis, brush bread slices with olive oil. Place on a baking sheet and bake in the oven until golden around the edges.

Pass gazpacho through a sieve and pour into individual martini glasses.

Garnish with red onion and parsley. Serve with crostinis and an assortment of olives.

Serves 8.

Difficulty 1.

Torched Cherry Sangria

1 lemon wedge
1 orange wedge
1 maraschino cherry
3 oz. (9 cl) Merlot
1/2 oz. (1.5 cl) BACARDI® TORCHED CHERRY™ flavored rum
1/2 oz. (1.5 cl) Cointreau
3/4 oz. (2 cl) orange juice
1/2 oz. (1.5 cl) simple syrup

Put lemon and orange wedges in a chilled tall glass. Fill with ice and add remaining ingredients. Stir to mix and garnish with a slice of orange.

Vintages

Paella de Marisco (Traditional Seafood, Meat and Saffron Rice Dish)

CHICKEN
1 tablespoon (15 g) sweet paprika
1 teaspoon (5 g) dried oregano
1/4 cup (60 ml) extra virgin olive oil
1 3-pound (1.35 kg) frying chicken,
cut into 10 pieces
Salt and freshly ground black pepper

PAELLA
2 tablespoons (30 ml) extra virgin olive oil
2 cloves garlic, peeled and chopped
1 yellow onion, peeled and chopped
2 shallots, peeled and chopped
1 red bell pepper, cubed
1 green bell pepper, cubed
3 cups (700 g) short grain Spanish rice
1/2 cup (120 ml) dry white wine
1 tablespoon (15 g) tomato paste
1 quart (1 L) water or chicken stock (page 156)
5 saffron threads
2 tomatoes, cubed
1/2 cup (115 g) frozen peas
1/3 cup olives, pitted and quartered

SEAFOOD
12 sea scallops
12 to 18 large shrimp, peeled,
deveined and tail on
1/2 pound (250 g) squid mix

GARNISH
Chopped parsley

EQUIPMENT
Chef's knife and cutting board
Large paella pan or large sauté pan
Medium glass or stainless steel bowl
Stirring spoon

For chicken, mix spices with 2 tablespoons (30 ml) olive oil in a small glass or stainless steel bowl. Rub chicken with spice mixture and refrigerate for 1 hour.

Heat remaining olive oil in a paella pan over medium-high heat and sauté marinated chicken, skin-side down first, on all sides until evenly browned. Season with salt and pepper. Remove from pan and reserve.

In the same pan, heat oil over medium-high heat. Add garlic, onion and shallots and sauté for 3 minutes or until onion is translucent. Add peppers and sauté for 5 minutes. Fold in rice and sir-fry to coat the grains with juices and oil. Deglaze with wine. Add tomato paste

and mix well. Pour in chicken stock, return chicken to pan and simmer for 10 minutes, gently moving the pan around so the rice cooks evenly and absorbs the liquid. Add saffron and tomatoes and simmer for 5 minutes. Add seafood and peas and simmer for another 8 minutes, shaking the pan often but without stirring. Add olives at the last minute.

Serve paella on warmed plates and finish with chopped parsley.

Serves 6.

Difficulty 3.

WINE PAIRING ⌒ PINOT NOIR, VIÑA CONO SUR, VISION, COLCHAGUA VALLEY, CHILE

Vintages

WINE PAIRING ❧ CODORNÍU, BRUT, CAVA, "CLÁSICO", RESERVA, SPAIN

Crema Catalán
(Cream Catalan)

Mus de Chocolate con Ron
(Chocolate Mousse)

CREAM CATALAN
1/4 cup (120 ml) orange juice

2 egg yolks
1/2 cup (115 g) granulated sugar
1/2 tablespoon (7.5 g) cornstarch
1 cinnamon stick
Zest of 1/2 orange
3/4 cup (180 ml) milk

CARAMEL
1/2 cup (115 g) granulated sugar
1/2 cup (120 ml) water
1 teaspoon (5 ml) lemon juice

GARNISH
1 6-ounce can (170 g) mandarins
in syrup, drained

EQUIPMENT
1 baking sheet
1 large glass or stainless steel bowl
1 rubber spatula
1 serving fork
1 wire whisk
3 small saucepans
6 small ramekins or aperitif glasses
Soup ladle
Wooden spoon

MOUSSE
1 cup (240 ml) heavy cream
10 ounces (235 g) bittersweet
chocolate chips
2 ounces espresso or strong coffee
2 tablespoons (30 ml) dark rum
2 tablespoons (30 g) unsalted butter

GARNISH
Whipped cream
Chocolate shavings
Chocolate accents, purchased

EQUIPMENT
6 ramekins or aperitif glasses
Hand mixer or wire whisk
Large glass or stainless steel bowl
Rubber spatula
Small saucepan
Stirring spoon

In a small saucepan over medium heat, bring orange juice to a boil and reduce by half.

Meanwhile, in a glass or stainless steel bowl, beat egg yolks and sugar until frothy. Add cornstarch, cinnamon stick, orange zest and milk and mix thoroughly. Pour mixture in a small saucepan; incorporate reduced orange juice and slowly heat, stirring constantly until it thickens.

Remove from heat, discard cinnamon stick and ladle mixture into ramekins. Allow to cool and refrigerate for 2 hours.

For caramel, place sugar and water in a small saucepan over medium heat and cook until caramel turns golden. Add lemon juice and remove from heat. Using a greased fork, take a small amount of caramel, drizzle on a greased baking sheet and gently form into a small airy ball. Create as many balls as necessary.

Garnish each cream Catalan with mandarins and a caramel ball.

Serves 6.

Difficulty 2.

Combine 3 tablespoons (45 ml) of heavy cream, chocolate, coffee, rum and butter in a small saucepan and melt over simmering water (bain-marie), stirring constantly. Remove from heat and let cool, stirring occasionally.

In a chilled glass bowl, using a hand mixer, beat remaining cream to soft peaks. Fold 1/4 of the whipped cream into the chocolate mixture to lighten it. Fold in the remaining whipped cream.

Spoon into glasses and chill for 2 hours.

Garnish with a dollop of whipped cream. Sprinkle with chocolate shavings and finish with chocolate accents.

Serves 6.

Difficulty 1.

Mus de Pistacho
(Pistachio Mousse)

MOUSSE
2 egg yolks
1/2 cup (115 g) granulated sugar
1 cup (240 ml) warm milk
1 teaspoon (5 ml) vanilla extract
1/3 cup (85 g) pistachio nuts, chopped
1 tablespoon (15 ml) Crème de Menthe
3/4 cup (180 ml) heavy cream

GARNISH
Chopped pistachio
6 white chocolate dessert half moons,
purchased
6 raspberries
Mint leaves

EQUIPMENT
6 ramekins or aperitif glasses
Chef's knife and cutting board
Hand mixer or wire whisk
Large glass or stainless steel bowl
Rubber spatula
Small saucepan

In a saucepan, beat egg yolks and sugar. Stir in milk and vanilla extract. Cook over low heat until mixture thickens, about 3 to 5 minutes.

Remove from heat; add chopped pistachios and crème de menthe and let cool, stirring constantly.

In a chilled glass bowl, using a hand mixer, beat cream to soft peaks. Fold 1/4 of the whipped cream into the pistachio mixture to lighten it. Fold in the remaining whipped cream.

Spoon into glasses and chill for 2 hours.

Sprinkle each mousse with chopped pistachio and garnish each mousse with a chocolate moon, a raspberry and mint leaf.

Serves 6.

Difficulty 1.

Torta de Queso y Fresas
(Strawberry Cheesecake)

STRAWBERRY COMPOTE
1 cup (230 g) strawberries, quartered
1 cup (230 g) granulated sugar
1 teaspoon (5 ml) vanilla extract
3 tablespoons (45 ml) water

CHEESECAKE
8 ounces (226 g) cream cheese
1/2 cup (115 g) granulated sugar
1/2 cup (120 ml) heavy cream

MERINGUE
2 egg whites, room temperature
1/4 cup (60 g) granulated sugar

GARNISH
6 wild strawberries

EQUIPMENT
2 large glass or stainless steel bowls
2 small saucepans
6 ramekins or aperitif glasses
Hand mixer or wire whisk
Rubber spatula

In a small saucepan over medium heat, combine all ingredients for the strawberry compote and bring to a boil. Lower heat and simmer for 15 minutes or until berries are soft and syrup is thickened.

Remove from heat, let cool, cover and refrigerate.

For cheesecake, in a small saucepan over medium heat, soften cream cheese and incorporate sugar.

In a chilled glass bowl, using a hand mixer, beat cream to soft peaks. Fold 1/4 of the whipped cream into the mixture to lighten it. Fold in the remaining whipped cream.

To make meringue, place egg whites in a stainless steel or glass bowl and, using a handheld mixer, beat on medium speed until soft peaks form. Gradually add sugar a little at a time until stiff peaks form.

Fold into the cheese mixture.

Fill each glass half way, spoon a small amount of strawberry compote and finish with another spoonful of cheese mixture. Refrigerate for 2 hours.

Garnish with a spoonful of strawberry compote and a wild strawberry.

Serves 6.

Difficulty 3.

Vintages

ROYAL CARIBBEAN'S SIGNATURE STEAKHOUSE, KNOWN FOR ITS GREAT STEAKS AND FRIENDLY, PROFESSIONAL SERVICE.

THE AMBIANCE AND DÉCOR IS INSPIRED BY A 1920S CHICAGO SCENE WITH A MURAL COMMISSIONED TO AN ARTIST WHOSE SPECIALTY IS TO CREATE BACKDROPS FOR POPULAR MOVIES SUCH AS "THE PIRATES OF THE CARIBBEAN" AND "CHARLIE WILSON'S WAR."

DECORATED IN DARK WOODS AND RICH BURGUNDY HUES, CHOPS EVOKES A '40S SWING-ERA STYLE, COMPLETE WITH FRANK SINATRA AND DEAN MARTIN MUSIC, CREATING A "RAT PACK" AMBIANCE OF A DIFFERENT AGE. ACCENTED WITH OVERSIZED CHAIRS, ROMANTIC LIGHTING AND TOUCHES OF CLASSIC ELEGANCE, CHOPS STEAKHOUSE FEATURES PREMIUM CUTS OF QUALITY STEAKS, FRESH SEAFOOD, HEARTY SIDE DISHES AND DECADENT DESSERTS.

CHOPS' OPEN GALLEY ALSO ALLOWS OUR GUESTS A DIRECT VIEW OF THE ACTION BEHIND THE SCENES.

You can choose to dine either in the elegant dining room or the cozy patio that opens into Central Park. Either way Chops Steakhouse is the perfect place for a romantic dinner or an encounter with friends.

Chops Grille

Spicy Tuna

PARMESAN TUILES

1/2 cup (115 g) salted butter,
room temperature
2 tablespoons (30 g) granulated sugar
Pinch of salt
2 egg whites
1/4 cup (60 g) all-purpose flour, sifted
3/4 cup (175 g) grated Parmesan cheese
2 tablespoons (30 g) black sesame seeds

SPICY TUNA

6 ounces (170 g) sushi/sashimi
grade tuna (maguro)
2 teaspoons (10 ml) Sriracha
hot chili sauce, purchased
2 teaspoons (10 ml) chili oil
2 teaspoons (10 ml) eel sauce (page 111)
Salt

SALSA

2 ripe avocadoes, peeled,
pit removed and diced small
1 English cucumber, peeled and diced small
Juice of 1 freshly squeezed lemon

GARNISH

Daikon sprouts
1/2 red bell pepper,
julienned and kept in ice water
1/2 yellow bell pepper,
julienned and kept in ice water
1/4 cup (60 ml) eel sauce (page 111)

EQUIPMENT

3 glass bowls
Chef's knives and cutting board
Cookie sheet
Paper towels
Parchment paper
Pizza cutter
Rolling pin
Soup spoon
Whisk
Wooden spoon

Preheat oven to 350°F or 180°C.

To make tuiles, whisk together butter, sugar, salt and egg whites in a glass bowl. Using a wooden spoon, fold in flour and Parmesan cheese.

Spread Parmesan batter on a cookie sheet lined with greased parchment paper. Cover mixture with another greased parchment paper and flatten using a rolling pin. Refrigerate for one hour.

Remove top layer of parchment paper from the chilled batter. Sprinkle chilled batter with sesame seeds and bake in the oven for 6 minutes.

Remove from oven and cut into rectangles using a pizza cutter.

Place back in the oven and bake for an additional 6 to 8 minutes or until tuiles are a golden brown color.

Remove from oven and let cool.

To make spicy tuna, mash tuna with the back of a spoon to remove the strings from the tuna loin, then dice. Place tuna on a plate lined with paper towels to remove excess water.

Mix Sriracha sauce, chili oil and eel sauce in a glass bowl. Add tuna to the marinade and stir. Season with salt to taste. Cover and refrigerate for 1 hour.

For salsa, mix avocado and cucumber with lemon juice in a glass bowl. Cover and refrigerate for 1 hour.

Arrange avocado cucumber salsa in the center of a chilled appetizer plate in a straight line. Top with two layers of tuile and spicy tuna. Garnish with daikon sprouts and bell pepper julienne. Drizzle with eel sauce.

Serves 6.

Difficulty 2.

Luxury Martini

2 oz. (6 cl) vodka or gin
1/4 oz. (0.75 cl) dry vermouth

Fill shaker with ice and add all ingredients. Shake well and strain into a chilled martini glass. Garnish with a lemon twist or pitted green olives.

Chops Grille

Beef Tenderloin and Eggplant Tower

LEMONGRASS OIL

2 stalks lemongrass, roughly cut
1 medium white onion, peeled and chopped
4 cloves garlic, peeled
1 bunch cilantro, roots only
1 medium size fresh gingerroot,
peeled and roughly cut
1 cup (240 ml) vegetable oil

CILANTRO CHILI DRESSING

5 limes, peeled and cored
4 cloves garlic, peeled and chopped
2 shallots, peeled and chopped
1/4 cup (60 ml) fish sauce
2 tablespoons (60 g) palm sugar
1/4 cup (60 ml) soy sauce
1/2 teaspoon (2.5 g) Tom Yum paste
1/2 cup (120 ml) chicken stock (page 156)
1/2 bunch fresh cilantro, chopped
2 fresh jalapeños, deseeded and chopped

EGGPLANT

2 tablespoons (60 ml) extra virgin olive oil
1 medium eggplant, thinly sliced
Salt and freshly ground black pepper

BEEF

1 pound (450 g) beef tenderloin, tail end cut
2 tablespoons (60 ml) vegetable oil

SALAD

8 ounces (230 g) mesclun mix
4 ounces (115 g) baby watercress
2 Belgium endives, cut in half and julienned
1/4 bunch cilantro leaves
1/2 red bell pepper, julienned and kept in iced water
1/2 green bell pepper, julienned and kept in iced water
2 scallions, green part only, julienned
20 snow peas, blanched, julienned and kept in iced water

GARNISH

Parsley sprigs

EQUIPMENT

2 ovenproof baking dishes
Blender or hand mixer
Chef's knife and cutting board
Grill pan or heavy skillet
Large glass or stainless steel bowl
Medium size heavy saucepan
Small glass or stainless steel bowl
Small saucepan
Wire mesh strainer
Wire whisk

Preheat oven to 400°F or 205°C.

For lemongrass oil, place all ingredients into a small saucepan, cover and simmer for 30 minutes or until all ingredients reach a golden color.

Allow to cool and strain using a small sieve. Oil will keep for 2 weeks once refrigerated.

To make cilantro dressing, place all ingredients into a blender and purée. Pass though a sieve into a stainless steel or glass bowl and add 1/4 cup of lemongrass oil. Mix well and keep cool.

Liberally brush beef tenderloin with half of the cilantro-lemongrass mixture and marinate for 2 hours.

Lightly oil a grill pan and heat over medium-high heat. Place eggplant slices on grill and cook each side for 2 minutes, turning only once. Season with salt and pepper and transfer to a baking dish. Cook in the oven for 5 to 7 minutes or until eggplant is soft.

Remove eggplant from the oven and brush with lemongrass oil. Allow to cool.

Meanwhile, warm a grill pan over high heat and sear tenderloin on all sides. Transfer to an ovenproof dish and roast in the oven for 10 to 12 minutes or until medium rare.

Remove from oven, cover and let rest on the side of the stove for 10 minutes. Cut in 1/4" thick slices.

In a large stainless steel or glass bowl, toss all salad ingredients with remaining cilantro dressing.

Place two eggplant slices in the center of chilled plates, top with half of the salad mix and 2 beef slices, then the remaining salad and 2 more beef slices. Garnish with parsley sprigs and drizzle with additional lemongrass oil.

Serves 6.

Difficulty 3.

Chops Salad

SALAD

12 baby beetroots, scrubbed clean
Salt and freshly ground black pepper
2 tablespoons (30 g) granulated sugar
2 tablespoons (30 g) unsalted butter

5 ounces (140 g) baby arugula lettuce
10 ounces (285 g) mesclun mix
4 plum tomatoes, washed and cut into wedges
8 hard boiled eggs, peeled and cut into wedges
12 strips bacon, baked until crisp
and cut into 1/2" pieces

VINAIGRETTE

1/2 cup (120 ml) extra virgin olive oil
8 shallots, peeled and halved
2 tablespoons (30 g) brown sugar
1/4 cup (60 ml) Cabernet wine
1/3 cup (90 ml) chicken stock (page 156)
1 teaspoon (15 g) Dijon mustard
1/4 cup (60 ml) red wine vinegar
Salt and freshly ground white pepper

GARNISH

Baby beetroot leaves

EQUIPMENT

Chef's knife and cutting board
Food processor or immersion blender
Medium sauté pan
Sieve
Small glass or stainless steel bowl
Small sauté pan
Stockpot
Wire mesh strainer
Wire whisk

Place beetroots in a large pot filled with hot water and seasoned with salt. Bring to a boil and cook for 20 minutes or until beetroots are cooked through.

Drain and refresh under cold water.

Peel beetroots with the back of a knife, cut into quarters, season with salt and pepper and sprinkle with sugar.

In a medium-sized sauté pan, melt butter over medium heat and sauté beetroots for 5 to 7 minutes or until caramelized.

For vinaigrette, in a small sauté pan over medium heat, warm 1 tablespoon olive oil and sauté shallots with brown sugar for 5 minutes. Deglaze with wine and reduce by half. Add chicken stock, bring to a boil, cover with aluminum foil and simmer for 15 minutes or until shallots are falling apart.

Strain liquid through a sieve and process shallots into a fine purée using a food processor. Combine liquid and shallot purée into a stainless steel or glass bowl and allow to cool.

Stir mustard into cooled shallot reduction, add vinegar and whisk in remaining olive oil. Adjust seasoning with salt and pepper.

Assemble lettuces on chilled plates. Garnish with tomatoes, eggs, bacon and baby caramelized beetroots. Drizzle with shallot vinaigrette and decorate with baby beetroot leaves.

Serves 8.

Difficulty 2.

Chops Grille

WINE PAIRING ⌒ SEQUOIA GROVE, NAPA, CALIFORNIA

Forest Mushroom Soup

SOUP

3 tablespoons (45 ml) extra virgin olive oil
1 clove garlic, peeled and chopped
2 medium yellow onions, peeled and diced
10 ounces (485 g) crimini mushrooms
10 ounces (485 g) button mushrooms
10 ounces (485 g) small portabella
mushrooms or 2 large mushrooms
2 large Idaho potatoes,
peeled and thickly sliced
1 sprig thyme
1 bay leaf
1/2 cup (120 ml) dry white wine
1 quart (1 L) vegetable stock (page 156)
Salt and freshly ground black pepper
1/4 cup (60 ml) heavy cream

GARNISH

4 ounces (120 g) enoki mushrooms
3 tablespoons (45 ml) white truffle oil

EQUIPMENT

2 large saucepans or medium size stockpots
Chef's knife and cutting board
Food processor or immersion blender
Ladle
Wooden spoon

In a large saucepan or medium size stockpot, over medium heat, warm oil and sauté garlic and onions for 4 minutes.

Add mushrooms, potatoes and herbs and sauté for 5 minutes, allowing potatoes to begin to caramelize.

Deglaze with white wine and add vegetable stock. Bring to a boil and simmer for 10 minutes or until potatoes are soft to the touch. Season with salt and pepper.

In batches, transfer mixture into a food processor and blend until smooth. Pour into a clean saucepan, add heavy cream and mix well. Taste, adjust seasoning if necessary and keep warm.

Ladle soup into warmed bowls, garnish with enoki mushrooms and a drizzle of truffle oil.

Serves 6.

Difficulty 1.

Pan-fried Barramundi

FONDANT POTATOES

6 medium Idaho potatoes pared
into rectangular blocks, then blanched
1/4 cup (60 g) salted butter
1 1/2 cups (360 ml) warm
chicken stock (page 156)
Salt and freshly ground black pepper

BUTTERNUT SQUASH PURÉE

1 butternut squash, peeled,
seeds removed and cut into large cubes
2 cups (480 ml) vegetable stock (page 156)
1/4 teaspoon (1.5 g) ground nutmeg
1/4 teaspoon (1.5 g) cinnamon powder
Pinch allspice powder
1/3 cup (90 ml) heavy cream
Salt and freshly ground white pepper

LIME BEURRE BLANC

1 tablespoon (15 ml) vegetable oil
2 shallots, peeled and minced
2 tablespoons (30 ml) white wine
1 tablespoon (15 ml) white wine vinegar
1/4 cup (60 ml) fish stock (page 156)
1/4 cup (60 ml) clam juice
1/4 cup (60 ml) heavy cream, reduced by half
1/2 pound (250 g) unsalted butter, cubed
Juice of 1 lime
Zest of 1 lime
Salt and freshly ground white pepper

FISH

6 7-ounce (200 g) fillets of barramundi,
halved lengthwise
Salt and freshly ground black pepper
2 tablespoons (30 ml) extra virgin olive oil

VEGETABLES

1/4 cup (60 g) tempura flour
2 tablespoons (30 ml) ice cold water
1 nori leaf, cut into 1/2-inch thick strips
6 baby carrots, peeled,
halved lengthwise and blanched
6 asparagus spears, trimmed and blanched
6 broccolini florets, trimmed and blanched
1/2 cup (120 ml) vegetable oil

SPINACH

1 tablespoon (15 g) salted butter
2 cloves garlic, peeled and minced
7 ounces (200 g) fresh spinach
Salt and freshly ground white pepper

EQUIPMENT

Bain-marie or double boiler
Blender
Chef's knives and cutting board
Colander
Fine sieve
Glass bowl
Large saucepan
Large sauté pan
Metal tongs
Ovenproof dish
Paper towels
Small sauté pan
Square baking dish
Whisk

Preheat oven to 320°F or 160°C.

Sauté potato blocks in melted butter in a large sauté pan over medium heat for 4 to 5 minutes or until potatoes acquire a little golden color. Transfer potatoes to a square baking dish and season with salt and pepper. Pour warm chicken stock over potatoes and bake in the oven for 15 to 18 minutes or until potatoes are tender.

Place butternut squash cubes and vegetable stock in a large saucepan and bring to a boil over high heat. Reduce heat to medium and simmer for 10 minutes or until squash is cooked throughout.

Drain squash using a colander and transfer to a blender. Add spices and heavy cream and blend until smooth. Return to saucepan and season to taste with salt and pepper. Keep warm.

To prepare beurre blanc, warm oil in a small sauté pan over medium heat and sauté shallots for 3 minutes or until translucent. Deglaze the pan with white wine. Add vinegar, fish stock and clam juice, bring to a boil and simmer for 10 minutes or until reduced by half.

Add cream and bring to a quick boil. Remove from heat and strain through a fine sieve into a glass bowl. Adjust seasoning with salt and pepper to taste. Whisk in butter a little at a time, then add lime juice and lime zest. Keep warm in a bain-marie or double boiler.

Pat barramundi fillets dry with paper towels and season them with salt and pepper. Warm olive oil in a large sauté pan over medium-high heat and sear the fish fillets for 1 minute on each side. Remove from pan and transfer to an ovenproof dish. Place in the oven to finish cooking for 4 to 5 minutes, or until fish fillets are cooked throughout.

While fish is cooking, place tempura flour in a small glass bowl and whisk in water. Do not over-mix.

Assemble vegetable bundles by wrapping a nori leaf strip around two halves of carrots, a stem of asparagus and a broccolini floret. Repeat until all the vegetables have been used.

Warm vegetable oil in a shallow saucepan over medium-high heat.

Lightly dip vegetable bundles in tempura batter and deep-fry in hot oil for 2 to 3 minutes, turning often with metal tongs, until batter is a light golden color. Remove bundles from oil and place on a plate lined with paper towels to drain excess oil.

In a sauté pan over medium heat, melt butter and sauté garlic for 2 minutes, but do not brown. Add spinach and cook for 1 minute or until wilted. Season with salt and pepper.

Place potato block off-center on a warmed entrée plate and top with wilted spinach on one corner and barramundi fillet on the other. Garnish with vegetable bundle. Finish with a few spoonfuls of butternut squash purée. Drizzle the fish and accompaniments with lime beurre blanc.

Serves 6.

Difficulty 3.

WINE PAIRING ☞ DOMAINE DENIS GAUDRY, POUILLY-FUMÉ, LOIRE, FRANCE

Chops Grille

Wine Pairing ⌒ Spring Valley, Meritage, "Uriah", Walla Walla, Washington

Beef Short Ribs

SHORT RIBS
8 beef short ribs, bone-in
Salt and freshly ground black pepper
1/4 cup (60 ml) extra virgin olive oil
1 large yellow onion, peeled and chopped
2 stalks celery, chopped
2 carrots, peeled and chopped
1 750-ml bottle Cabernet wine
1 1/2 quarts (1.4 L) veal or
beef stock (page 157)

MASHED POTATOES
2 pounds (900 g) Yukon Gold potatoes,
peeled and quartered
3/4 cup (175 ml) heavy cream
2 tablespoons (30 g) unsalted butter
Salt and freshly ground white pepper

GRILLED TOMATOES
4 Roma tomatoes, halved
2 tablespoons (30 ml) extra virgin olive oil
Salt and freshly ground black pepper

BROCCOLINI
1 tablespoon (15 g) butter
1 bunch broccolini, trimmed or 1 head broccoli,
cut into florets, steamed and refreshed in
ice water
Salt and freshly ground black pepper

GARNISH
Baby watercress

EQUIPMENT
Baking dish
Chef's knife and cutting board
Ladle
Large sauté pan
Metal tongs
Ovenproof baking dish or Dutch oven
Potato ricer
Small sauté pan
Stockpot

Preheat oven to 350°F or 180°C.

Season ribs with salt and pepper.

In a large, heavy bottomed ovenproof pan over high heat, warm oil and brown ribs, in batches, on all sides. Transfer ribs to a plate as you work.

Using the same pan, reduce heat to medium and sauté onions, celery and carrots for 5 minutes. Pour off excess fat and deglaze with wine, scraping any bits from the bottom of the pan.

Reduce wine for 15 minutes or until thick and syrupy in consistency.

Return ribs to pan and add stock and enough water to cover the ribs. Bring to a boil, cover and braise in the oven for 2 to 2 1/2 hours or until meat is tender and easily separates from the bone. Allow ribs to cool in the liquid. Cover and refrigerate overnight.

The next day, remove solidified excess fat and return to medium heat, uncovered. Cook for 1 hour or until liquid has reduced by three quarters, frequently spooning sauce over ribs to keep them moist.

For mashed potatoes, place potatoes into salted cold water, bring to a boil and cook until potatoes are easily pierced with the tip of a knife, about 15 minutes. Drain and press potatoes through a potato ricer into a heated bowl. Stir in cream and butter. Adjust seasoning with salt and pepper. Set aside and keep warm.

Drizzle tomatoes with olive oil and season with salt and pepper. Using a small sauté pan over high heat, mark each tomato half and transfer into a small sheet pan. Finish cooking in the oven for 10 minutes.

For broccolini, in a large sauté pan over medium heat, melt butter and sauté vegetables for 3 minutes, or until warm. Season with salt and pepper.

Arrange a spoonful of mashed potatoes in the center of warmed plates. Top with a short rib and garnish with watercress sprig. Complement each plate with a grilled tomato, broccolini florets and a drizzle of sauce.

Serves 8.

Difficulty 4.

Chops Grille

Red Velvet Cake

SIMPLE SYRUP
1/4 cup (60 g) granulated sugar
1/3 cup (90 ml) water

CREAM CHEESE FROSTING
1 cup (235 g) unsalted butter,
    room temperature
1 1/2 cups (350 g) cream cheese,
    room temperature
4 cups (920 g) confectioner's sugar
1 teaspoon (5 ml) vanilla extract

RED VELVET CAKE
2 1/2 cups (580 g) all-purpose flour
2 tablespoons (30 g) unsweetened cocoa powder
2 teaspoons (10 g) baking powder
1/2 teaspoon (2.5 g) baking soda
1/2 teaspoon (2.5 g) salt
1/2 cup (120 ml) buttermilk or milk
1/2 cup (120 ml) vegetable oil
1 teaspoon (5 ml) red gel paste food coloring
1 teaspoon (5 ml) vanilla extract
1/2 cup (115 g) unsalted butter, softened
1 cup (235 g) sugar
3 eggs

GANACHE
1/4 cup (60 g) dark chocolate, broken into pieces
1/4 cup (60 ml) heavy cream

GARNISH
Dark chocolate chips
Mini white pearl sprinkles

EQUIPMENT
2 9-inch (23 cm) round cake pans
2 slotted spoons
2 small glass or stainless steel bowls
2 small saucepans
Chef's knife and cutting board
Large glass or stainless steel bowl
Long serrated knife
Metal spatula
Pastry brush
Piping or pastry bag
Rubber spatula
Small round piping tip
Stand mixer or hand mixer
Wire rack

Preheat oven to 350°F or 180°C.

Prepare syrup by mixing all ingredients in a small saucepan and boiling until sugar has melted. Let cool.

For cream cheese frosting, beat butter and cream cheese in a large bowl with an electric mixer set at medium-high speed, for 3 minutes or until fluffy. Reduce speed to medium and slowly add confectioner's sugar, 1/2 cup (115 g) at a time. Scrape sides of bowl with a rubber spatula and beat well after each addition. Then add vanilla and beat at medium speed for 1 minute more or until frosting is smooth.

Frosting may be prepared up to four days in advance and refrigerated in an airtight container. Before using, bring to room temperature and beat for about 5 minutes on low speed or until smooth.

To make cake, combine flour, cocoa powder, baking powder, baking soda and salt in a medium-sized bowl and whisk together.

In a small bowl, combine buttermilk, vegetable oil, red gel paste food coloring and vanilla extract and mix well.

In a medium bowl, with an electric mixer at medium speed, beat butter and sugar for about 4 minutes until creamy and light in color. Incorporate eggs, one at a time, beating well. Reduce mixer speed to low and slowly add flour mixture and buttermilk mixture. Beat for 2 minutes or until well mixed, scraping the sides of the bowl often with a rubber spatula.

Grease two 9-inch (23 cm) round cake pans.

Spoon batter into cake pans and bake for 25 to 30 minutes or until a toothpick inserted in the center of the cakes comes out clean.

Remove cakes from the baking pan and let cool on a wire rack for 30 minutes.

For ganache, warm chocolate and cream in a small saucepan over low heat until chocolate has melted. Stir well and set aside to cool.

Using a long serrated knife, slice each cake in half, horizontally. Place one of the cake layers, cut side facing up, onto your serving platter and brush with sugar syrup. Cover the cake layer with frosting. Place another layer of cake on top of the frosting and brush with sugar syrup, frost, stack and repeat, finishing with a rounded side as the top layer.

Using the metal spatula, spread cream cheese frosting on the sides and finish by frosting the top layer.

Spoon warm ganache into a piping or pastry bag or plastic sandwich bag fitted with a small, round tip. Drizzle chocolate across the top of the cake. Sprinkle with dark chocolate chips and mini white pearl sprinkles.

Dip a pastry brush into remaining ganache and brush across chilled desert plates in a horizontal line. Cut cake into slices and arrange on plates. Garnish with a chocolate cigarette.

Serves 8 to 10.

Difficulty 3.

Café Blanco

1 1/2 oz. (4.5 cl) Bailey's Irish Cream
1/2 oz. (1.5 cl) Monin Vanilla syrup
Piping hot coffee
Whipped cream

Pour Bailey's Irish Cream and vanilla syrup in an Irish coffee mug. Fill with coffee and top with a rosette of whipped cream.

Chops Grille

CASUAL AND CONTEMPORARY, IZUMI RESTAURANT AND SUSHI BAR IS A STYLISH ASIAN BISTRO DECORATED WITH BAMBOO, LIGHT WOOD AND DELICATE WATER LILIES. IT OFFERS A SEA-VIEW VISTA, RELAXING ATMOSPHERE AND JAPANESE-INFLUENCED MENU ITEMS CREATED WITH THE HELP OF CHEF CONSULTANT TRAVIS KAMIYAMA.

WORKING IN TANDEM WITH CHEF TRAVIS, ONE OF LOS ANGELES' MOST RECOGNIZED SUSHI CHEFS, OWNER OF SEVERAL SUCCESSFUL RESTAURANTS AND RENOWNED SUSHI INSTRUCTOR IN

CALIFORNIA, WE CREATED A TANTALIZING JAPANESE-STYLE CUISINE INCLUDING EXPERTLY CRAFTED SUSHI, SIZZLING HOT ROCK® AND SIMMERING SUKYIAKI.

SIT AT THE SUSHI BAR TO WATCH OUR SUSHI CHEF OR "ITAMAE" PREPARE HIS DELECTABLE CREATIONS; SIP A REFRESHING SAKE MARTINI SERVED BY A WAIT STAFF CLAD IN TRADITIONAL JAPANESE-INSPIRED BLACK-DRESS KIMONOS FROM THE TAISHO PERIOD (1912-1925), RELAX AND ENJOY THE BEST SUSHI ON THE SEVEN SEAS.

Izumi

Salmon Salad with White Sesame Dressing

SESAME DRESSING
1/4 cup (60 g) white sesame seeds, toasted
1/4 cup (60 g) granulated sugar
3 teaspoons (45 ml) dark soy sauce
1/2 cup bonito stock (page 114)
2 tablespoons (30 ml) ponzu sauce (page 111)
1 teaspoon (5 ml) chili sesame oil

SALAD
1 pound (450 g) salmon, skinless and cubed
3 ounces (85 g) masago
4 ounces (120 g) sprouts
6 ounces (170 g) mesclun
2 ounces (60 g) baby watercress
2 ounces (60 g) frisée lettuce
2 cucumbers, seeded and sliced lengthwise

GARNISH
1 tablespoon (15 g) black sesame seeds
4 teaspoons (20 g) tobiko

EQUIPMENT
2 small glass or stainless steel bowls
Chef's knife and cutting board
Large glass or stainless steel bowl
Small sauté pan

Toast sesame seeds by heating a small sauté pan over low heat and gently tossing seeds until they acquire a golden color. Immediately transfer seeds to small glass or stainless steel bowl and let cool.

For dressing, mix all ingredients in a small stainless steel or glass bowl.

In a large stainless steel or glass bowl, combine all ingredients for the salad and toss with dressing.

Arrange salad in chilled bowls, sprinkle with sesame seeds and garnish with a spoonful of tobiko.

Serves 4.

Difficulty 1.

Lychee Martini

1 1/2 oz. (4.5 cl) ABSOLUT®
1/2 oz. (1.5 cl) Monin Blue Lychee syrup
1/2 oz. (1.5 cl) pineapple juice

Fill shaker with ice and add all ingredients. Shake well and strain into a chilled martini glass. Garnish with a lychee.

Izumi

Tuna Carpaccio

GARLIC CHIPS

3 tablespoons (45 ml) extra virgin olive oil
4 cloves garlic, peeled and thickly shaved

AIOLI

1 teaspoon (5 g) Dijon mustard
2 cloves garlic, peeled and minced
1 egg
1 egg yolk
*1 tablespoon (15 ml) freshly squeezed
lemon juice*
1 cup (240 ml) extra virgin olive oil
Salt and freshly ground white pepper
1 teaspoon (5 g) wasabi powder

TUNA

*2 10-ounce (285 g) ahi tuna blocks
(sashimi grade)*
1 tablespoon (15 ml) extra virgin olive oil
Freshly ground black pepper

GARNISH

*1 jalapeño pepper, deseeded,
halved and thinly sliced*
3 ounces (85 g) tobiko
1 ounce (30 g) daikon sprouts

EQUIPMENT

Baking sheet
Chef's knife and cutting board
Food processor or blender
Pastry brush
Slotted spoon
Small glass bowl
Small saucepan
Spatula

In a small saucepan over low heat, warm oil and cook garlic for 8 minutes or until golden brown. Using a slotted spoon, transfer garlic chips into a plate lined with absorbent paper.

For aioli, in a blender, combine the mustard, garlic, eggs and lemon juice and purée. With the machine running, slowly add the olive oil a little at a time. Season with salt and pepper and add wasabi powder. Transfer into glass bowl, cover and refrigerate.

Using a sharp knife, cut tuna in 1-inch (2.5 cm) thin slices. Brush each slice with olive oil and sprinkle with black pepper.

Arrange tuna slices on chilled plates. Place a dollop of aioli on each tuna slice and garnish with jalapeño and a small mount of tobiko.

Top each tuna slice with a few garlic chips and finish decorating the plates with daikon sprouts.

Serves 6.

Difficulty 2.

Shrimp Wonton Soup

SHRIMP WONTON
2 teaspoons (10 ml) vegetable oil
1 shallot, minced
1 teaspoon (5 g) grated ginger
8 ounces (230 g) flounder fillets
1 egg white
1 tablespoon (15 g) cornstarch,
dissolved in 1 tablespoon (15 ml) water
1 teaspoon (5 ml) sake
1 teaspoon (5 ml) mirin sauce
Salt
18 medium shrimp, peeled,
deveined, tails off and chopped
18 square wonton wrappers
1 egg, beaten

BROTH
1 quart (1 L) chicken stock (page 156)
1 tablespoon (15 g) shredded ginger
2 scallions, halved
4 ounces (120 g) shiitake mushrooms, quartered
10 ounces (285 g) clear cellophane noodles,
soaked in water for 5 minutes and drained

GARNISH
2 green onions, sliced into thin rings

EQUIPMENT
Chef's knife and cutting board
Food processor
Large pot or stockpot
Medium glass bowl
Medium saucepan
Pastry brush
Slotted spoon
Small glass or stainless steel bowl
Small saucepan

To make wontons, in a small saucepan over medium heat, warm oil and sauté shallot and ginger for 5 minutes.

Place trimmed fish in a food processor and pulse until well-chopped, add egg white, cornstarch, sake, mirin, shallot mixture. Season with salt and mix to a smooth paste. Transfer into a glass bowl and fold in chopped shrimp.

Lightly brush wrappers with beaten egg. Place a spoonful of fish mousse in each wrapper and fold over diagonally, enclosing the mousse to form a triangle. Press the edges of the wrapper to seal. Fold in the 2 corners furthest apart, brush with some beaten egg and press together to seal.

Steam wontons for 5 minutes.

Meanwhile warm chicken stock, ginger, scallions and shiitake mushrooms over medium heat in a large stockpot. Bring to a boil and simmer for 5 minutes. Add cellophane noodles and simmer for 2 minutes or until noodles are warmed through.

To serve, place 3 shrimp wontons in individual warmed bowls, pour in the hot broth and noodles and garnish with green onion rings.

Serves 6.

Difficulty 3.

Izumi

WINE PAIRING ～ TYKU BLACK SUPER PREMIUM JUNAMI GINJO, SAKE

Foundation and Sauce Recipes

SUSHI RICE
2 cups (465 g) short-grain rice (also called shari)
2 cups (475 ml) water

SUSHI RICE VINEGAR
1/2 cup (120 ml) rice vinegar
1 tablespoon (15 g) sea salt
2 teaspoons (10 ml) mirin sauce
1/4 cup (60 g) granulated sugar
1 1/2-inch (4 cm) sheet kombu

To make sushi rice, rinse and rub the grains in cold water several times until the water turns from cloudy to clear.

Drain well and transfer to a large saucepan or stockpot. Let stand for 5 minutes. Add water and bring to a boil over high heat. Boil for 1 minute. Reduce heat to low and cook for 5 minutes.

Remove from heat and let rice sit for 15 minutes.

Meanwhile, in a saucepan over medium heat, simmer 1/3 cup (90 ml) rice vinegar, sea salt, mirin and sugar. Do not boil. Add kombu, remove from heat and allow to cool. Stir in remaining rice vinegar.

Transfer cooked rice into a wooden Japanese rice tub (Hangiri) or large glass bowl. Pour 3/4 of the rice vinegar mixture over the rice and mix quickly, while the rice is still hot, with a flat wooden spoon, using a slicing motion. Allow to cool.

Difficulty 2.

HAND VINEGAR
1 cup (240 ml) cold water
2 tablespoons (30 ml) rice vinegar

Mix all ingredients in a medium size glass or stainless steel bowl. Reserve in a glass jar and refrigerate.

SPICY JAPANESE MAYONNAISE
2 egg yolks
1/2 teaspoon (2.5 g) salt
Freshly ground white pepper
1 teaspoon (5 g) Dijon mustard
2 teaspoons (10 ml) rice vinegar
1 cup (240 ml) vegetable oil
1 teaspoon (5 ml) chili oil
1 teaspoon (5 g) wasabi powder

Make mayonnaise by beating the egg yolks with a whisk in a small stainless steel or glass bowl, adding the salt, pepper, mustard and rice vinegar, then gradually incorporating the vegetable oil a little at a time. Stir in chili oil and wasabi powder. Cover and chill.

WASABI
3 tablespoons (45 g) powdered wasabi
1 tablespoon (15 ml) water

Add water to wasabi powder in a small glass or stainless steel bowl a little at a time until it reaches a thick paste consistency.

EEL SAUCE
1/2 cup (120 ml) fish stock* (page 156)
1/2 cup (120 ml) soy sauce
1/2 cup (115 g) granulated sugar
1/2 cup (120 ml) mirin (Japanese sweet cooking wine)
1/4 cup (60 ml) sake

Heat all ingredients in a small saucepan over medium heat. Bring to a boil, reduce heat and simmer for 45 minutes, stirring often or until mixture has reduced by half.

Let cool and transfer to a stainless steel or glass bowl. Cover and refrigerate.

*Replace the saltwater fish heads and bones in the fish stock recipe on page 156 with eel heads and bones.

YUZU KOSHO RELISH
2 tablespoons (30 ml) yuzu kosho, purchased
2 cloves garlic, peeled and chopped
2 tablespoons (30 g) finely chopped fresh ginger
2 stalks lemongrass, chopped (tender part only)
1/2 bunch fresh cilantro, finely chopped
3 green onions, chopped
1/2 cup (120 ml) extra virgin olive oil

Mix all ingredients in a small stainless steel or glass bowl.

Cover and refrigerate overnight.

PONZU SAUCE
1/4 cup (60 ml) soy sauce
1/2 cup (120 ml) rice vinegar
2 tablespoons (30 ml) freshly squeezed lemon juice
3/4-inch (2 cm) square piece of kombu, wiped clean
1 ounce bonito flakes

Mix all ingredients in a stainless steel or glass bowl. Cover and refrigerate overnight. Strain and reserve in a glass bottle.

Difficulty for sauces 1.

EQUIPMENT FOR RICE
Flat wooden spoon
Glass bowl
Saucepan
Stockpot
Wooden Japanese rice tub

EQUIPMENT FOR SAUCES
2 small glass or stainless steel bowls
3 medium glass or stainless steel bowls
Chef's knife and cutting board
Sieve or cheesecloth
Small stirring spoons
Wire whisk
Wooden spoon

Izumi

Spider Roll

SOFT SHELL CRAB

1 5-ounce (140 g) soft shell crab, cleaned
Salt and freshly ground black pepper
2 tablespoons (30 g) potato starch
or all-purpose flour
2 tablespoons (30 ml) vegetable oil

ROLLS

1/2 sheet nori seaweed
2 ounces (60 g) sushi rice (page 111)
1 ounce (30 g) white sesame seeds
2 asparagus spears, blanched
1 cucumber, peeled, seeded and julienned
1 avocado, peeled, pitted,
cut in half and thinly sliced
1 ounce (30 g) daikon sprouts
1 ounce (30 g) spicy Japanese
mayonnaise (page 111)

GARNISH

Sasa bamboo leaf (optional)
1 ounce (30 g) masago eggs, purchased
1 ounce (30 g) eel sauce (page 111)

EQUIPMENT

Chef's knife and cutting board
Glass bowl
Makisu bamboo roller mat
Paper towels
Plastic wrap
Sauté pan
Sharp sushi knife
Slotted spoon

Season crab with salt and pepper. Place potato starch or flour in a glass bowl. Dredge crab in potato starch or flour, shaking off the excess.

Warm vegetable oil in a sauté pan over high heat. Place crab, top side down in pan and cook for 3 minutes, gently pressing body and legs against the pan. Turn crab over; cook an additional 3 minutes. Remove using a slotted spoon. Allow pieces to drain on a plate lined with paper towels.

Cut crab in half lengthwise, leaving legs attached.

To make the roll, spread makisu bamboo mat flat on a work surface and cover with plastic wrap. Lay nori sheet over plastic wrap and, using your hands, spread evenly with sushi rice, except for a half-inch border at the top and bottom. Keep your fingers and palms moistened with hand vinegar (page 111) so the rice doesn't stick to them. Sprinkle rice with sesame seeds and press gently to allow seed to adhere to rice.

Flip the sheet of rice-covered nori over so the rice is facing down. Place asparagus spear horizontally in the center of the roll, followed by a small amount of cucumber julienne, avocado slices, daikon sprouts (sticking out), a streak of spicy mayonnaise and soft shell crab, allowing its legs to extend over the long sides of the nori.

Lift the end of the nori nearest you and carefully roll it over the filling, pressing down as you go.

Roll bamboo mat forward, pressing the ingredients inside the cylinder shaped sushi. Keep the roll as tight as possible. Press the bamboo mat firmly with your hands, then remove the rolled sushi.

Slice roll into 5 pieces and arrange on a small platter covered with a Sasa bamboo leaf.

Garnish each roll with a spoonful of masago eggs and drizzle with eel sauce.

Serve with pickled ginger and wasabi.

Makes 5 pieces.

Difficulty 1.

Surf and Turf Roll

STEAK

5 ounces (140 g) beef filet
Salt and freshly ground black pepper
1 tablespoon (15 ml) vegetable oil

LOBSTER TEMPURA

1/4 cup (60 g) tempura batter mix,
purchased
1/4 cup (60 g) all-purpose flour, sifted
1 cup (240 ml) vegetable oil, for frying
1 5-ounce (140 g) lobster tail, poached,
chilled, shell removed and cut in half
lengthwise

ROLLS

1/2 sheet nori seaweed
3 ounces (85 g) sushi rice (page 111)
2 small avocadoes, peeled,
pitted, cut in half and thinly sliced

1 ounce (30 g) spicy mayonnaise (page 111)
1 ounce (30 ml) yuzu kosho relish (page 111)
1 ounce (30 ml) ponzu sauce (page 111)

GARNISH

Pickled ginger, purchased
Wasabi (page 111)

EQUIPMENT

Cast iron skillet or
heavy-bottom frying pan
Chef's knife and cutting board
Glass or stainless steel bowl
Makisu bamboo roller mat
Paper towels
Plastic wrap
Sharp sushi knife
Slotted spoon

Season steak with salt and pepper. Preheat broiler for 5 minutes on high heat. Broil to the desired degree of doneness, about 6 minutes for rare and 10 minutes for medium. Transfer to a platter, tent loosely with aluminum foil and let stand for 10 minutes. Transfer to a clean plate, cover and refrigerate.

Prepare tempura mix according to the instructions on the package.

Pour flour in a small glass bowl. Dredge lobster in flour and shake off any excess.

Dip each piece of lobster into the tempura batter and fry in hot oil until golden. Remove from frying pan using a slotted spoon, then place on a plate lined with paper towels to drain.

To make the roll, spread makisu bamboo mat flat on a work surface and cover with plastic wrap. Lay nori sheet over plastic wrap and, and using your hands, spread evenly with sushi rice. Keep your fingers and palms moistened with hand vinegar (page 111) so the rice doesn't stick to them.

Flip the sheet of rice-covered nori over so the rice is facing down. Place slices of avocado horizontally in the center of the roll, arrange lobster pieces alongside, allowing the very end of the tails to hang over the edge. Top with a streak of spicy Japanese mayonnaise.

Lift the end of the nori nearest you and carefully roll it over the filling, pressing down as you go.

Roll bamboo mat forward, pressing the ingredients inside the cylinder shaped sushi. Keep the roll as tight as possible. Press the bamboo mat firmly with your hands, then remove the rolled sushi.

Cut steak diagonally into thin slices and top roll with the strips of meat. Slice the finished roll into 6 to 8 pieces.

Spoon a small amount of yuzu kosho relish atop each sushi piece and drizzle with ponzu sauce. Serve with pickled ginger and wasabi.

Makes 6 to 8 pieces.

Difficulty 1.

Temari Sushi

TEMARI

3 ounces (85 g) sushi rice (page 111)
1 ounce (30 g) fresh salmon, thinly sliced
1 ounce (30 g) yellow tail, thinly sliced
1 ounce (30 g) sushi grade tuna,
thinly sliced
1 ounce (30 g) unagi
(broiled fresh water eel), sliced

GARNISH

1 jalapeño, slivered
1 teaspoon (5 g) lump fish eggs
1 teaspoon (5 g) white sesame seeds
1 teaspoon (5 g) yellow tomato,
small diced
Pickled ginger, purchased
Wasabi (page 111)

EQUIPMENT

Chef's knife and cutting board
Plastic wrap
Sharp sushi knife

To make temari, roll a small amount of rice into a ball, keeping your hands moistened with hand vinegar (page 111) so that the rice doesn't stick. Make additional balls until all the rice has been used.

Top each rice ball with a dot of wasabi then a slice of fish. Cover each ball with a small piece of plastic wrap and gently twist the wrap at the bottom to shape temari into a perfect ball.

Garnish each temari with a different ingredient. Transfer to a small platter and serve with soy sauce, pickled ginger and wasabi.

Makes 6 pieces.

Difficulty 1.

Orange Dragon Roll

SPICY TUNA

3 ounces (85 g) sushi/sashimi
grade tuna (maguro)
1 teaspoon (5 ml) Sriracha
hot chili sauce, purchased
1/2 teaspoon (2.5 g) masago
(smelt egg), purchased
1/2 teaspoon (2.5 ml) chili oil

ROLLS

1 sheet colored soy paper
3 ounces (85 g) sushi rice (page 111)
1 asparagus spear, blanched
1 ounce (30 g) sashimi grade salmon,
thinly sliced

To prepare the spicy tuna filling, chop tuna and mix with Sriracha hot chili sauce, masago and chili oil in a small glass bowl. Cover and refrigerate.

To make the roll, spread makisu bamboo mat flat on a work surface and cover with plastic wrap. Place soy paper on top of the plastic wrap and spread evenly with sushi rice using your hands. Keep your fingers and palms moistened with hand vinegar (page 111) so the rice doesn't stick to them.

Flip the rice-spread sheet of soy paper over so the rice is facing down. Place asparagus spear horizontally in the center of the roll and spread tuna alongside.

Lift the end of the soy paper nearest you and carefully roll it over the filling, pressing down as you go.

GARNISH

1 green onion, thinly chopped
Soy sauce
Eel sauce (page 111)
Pickled ginger, purchased
Wasabi (page 111)

EQUIPMENT

Makisu bamboo roller
Medium glass bowl
Plastic wrap
Sharp sushi knife and cutting board
Slotted spoon
Wooden or steel skewers

Roll bamboo mat forward, pressing the ingredients inside the cylinder-shaped sushi. Keep the roll as tight as possible. Press the bamboo mat firmly with your hands, and then remove the rolled sushi.

Carefully place salmon slices across the top of the roll.

Wrap roll with a clean piece of plastic wrap and gently reshape using the bamboo mat. Slice roll into 6 to 8 pieces.

Garnish with chopped green onions and serve with soy sauce, eel sauce, pickled ginger and wasabi.

Makes 6 to 8 pieces.

Difficulty 2.

Vegetarian Roll

ROLLS

2 ounces (60 g) sushi rice (page 111)
1 ounce (30 g) black sesame seeds
2 asparagus spears, blanched
1 cucumber, peeled, seeded and julienned
1 avocado, peeled, pitted,
cut in half and thinly sliced
1 red bell pepper, julienned
1 yellow bell pepper, julienned
1 ounce (30 g) spicy Japanese mayonnaise
(page 111)

GARNISH

Sasa bamboo leaf (optional)
Pickled ginger, purchased
Wasabi (page 111)
Soy sauce, purchased

EQUIPMENT

Chef's knife and cutting board
Makisu bamboo roller mat
Plastic wrap
Sharp sushi knife

To make the roll, spread makisu bamboo mat flat on a work surface and cover with plastic wrap. Using your hands, spread sushi rice evenly on plastic wrap. Keep your fingers and palms moistened with hand vinegar (page 111) so the rice doesn't stick to them. Sprinkle rice with black sesame seeds and press gently to allow seeds to adhere to rice.

Flip the sheet of rice over so the sesame seeds are facing down. Place asparagus spears horizontally in the center of the roll, followed by a small amount of cucumber julienne, avocado slices, julienne bell peppers and a streak of spicy mayonnaise.

Roll bamboo mat forward, pressing the ingredients inside the cylinder shaped sushi. Keep the roll as tight as possible. Press the bamboo mat firmly with your hands, then remove the rolled sushi.

Slice roll into 5 pieces and arrange on a small platter covered with a Sasa bamboo leaf.

Serve with pickled ginger, wasabi and soy sauce.

Makes 5 pieces.

Difficulty 1.

Izumi

Seafood Sukiyaki

BONITO STOCK

*1 20-inch (50 cm) length kelp,
thoroughly wiped*
2.2 quarts (2 L) cold water
3 cups (60 to 80 g) bonito flakes
1/2 cup (120 ml) light soy sauce
1/4 cup (60 ml) mirin sauce
2 tablespoons (30 ml) sake

INGREDIENTS

8 ounces (230 g) salmon, sliced sashimi style
*8 ounces (230 g) dolphin fish or sea bream,
sliced sashimi style*
8 sea scallops
*8 large shrimp, peeled,
deveined, tail on*
4 ounces (120 g) enoki mushrooms
*4 ounces (120 g) shiitake mushrooms,
washed and stems removed*
1 small Chinese cabbage, leaves blanched
4 ounces (120 g) snow peas, blanched
*3 large carrots, peeled,
cut diagonally and blanched*
*1 block (10-ounce) (285 g) regular tofu,
cut into large cubes*
*8 ounces (230 g) cellophane noodles,
soaked in water for 5 minutes and drained*
1 bunch young celery leaves
1 ounce (30 g) white sesame seeds

EQUIPMENT

2 large pots or stockpots
Chef's knife and cutting board
Fine mesh strainer or Chinois
Nabe pot
Soup ladle
Wooden spoon

For stock, place kelp and 2 quarts of cold water into a stockpot over medium-low heat, and slowly bring to a simmer. Regulate heat so that the water takes approximately 10 minutes to reach a boil.

Remove kelp, add remaining cold water and bonito flakes and quickly bring to a boil.

Remove from heat and skim the surface. Allow bonito flakes to sink to the bottom, about 1 minute and strain liquid through a fine mesh strainer into a large stockpot.

Incorporate the soy sauce, mirin sauce and sake. Return to heat and keep to a simmer.

Arrange all the ingredients in a Nabe pot. Pour in simmering stock, cover and bring to a boil. Cook for 10 minutes and serve with a side dish of rice garnished with white sesame seeds (recipe page 118).

Serves 4.

Difficulty 1.

WINE PAIRING ❦ RÉMY PANNIER, VOUVRAY, FRANCE

Izumi

Vegetable Tempura

TENTSYU DIPPING SAUCE
1 cup (240 ml) bonito sauce, purchased
3 tablespoons (45 ml) dark soy sauce
3 tablespoons (45 ml) mirin sauce
1/3 cup (85 g) shredded daikon radish

VEGETABLES
1/2 cup (115 g) tempura batter mix, purchased
1 cup (140 ml) vegetable oil, for frying
1/2 cup (115 g) all-purpose flour, sifted
18 green asparagus spears, peeled
2 sweet potatoes, peeled and sliced
2 white onions, peeled and thickly sliced
2 zucchini, thickly sliced
2 large carrots, peeled and diagonally sliced
6 large shiitake mushrooms

EQUIPMENT
2 medium glass or stainless steel bowls
Cast iron skillet or heavy-bottomed frying pan
Chef's knife and cutting board
Paper towels
Slotted spoon
Wire whisk

To make dipping sauce, mix first 3 ingredients in a small stainless steel or glass bowl.

Prepare tempura mix according to the instructions on the package.

For the tempura vegetables, warm oil in a frying pan over medium-high heat.

Dredge vegetables in flour and shake off any excess. Dip each piece into the tempura batter and deep-fry in the hot vegetable oil until golden. Drain and place on paper towels.

Arrange vegetables on warmed plates. Serve with lukewarm tentsyu dipping sauce garnished with a tablespoon (15g) of shredded daikon.

Serves 6.

Difficulty 1.

Hot Rock®

LEMON-GINGER VINAIGRETTE
2 tablespoons (30 ml) lemon juice
2 tablespoons (30 ml) lime juice
3 tablespoons (45 ml) rice vinegar
1 clove garlic, minced
1 teaspoon grated ginger
1 small stalk lemongrass, split open
1/3 cup (90 ml) sweet chili sauce

SWEET SOY SAUCE
1/4 cup (60 g) granulated sugar
3 tablespoons (45 ml) sake
1 cup (240 ml) light soy sauce

SWEET CHILI SAUCE
Sweet Thai chili sauce, purchased

STEAMED RICE
2 cups Japanese-style rice
2 1/4 (540 ml) cups water

HOT ROCK
6 7-ounce (200 g) beef tenderloin filets,
cut into 1/2-inch slices
1 broccoli rapini, cut into florets and blanched
6 baby bok choy, blanched
12 crimini mushrooms, cleaned and stems
removed
2 carrots, peeled, julienned and blanched
5 ounces (140 g) bean sprouts

EQUIPMENT
2 small saucepans
6 ceramic ramekins or small serving bowls
6 Hot Rock® Grills – purchased
Chef's knife and cutting board
Colander
Rice cooker (optional)
Serving platter

For the ginger vinaigrette, in a small saucepan over medium heat, warm lemon juice, lime juice and rice vinegar. Add garlic, ginger and lemongrass and simmer for 5 minutes. Remove from heat. Discard lemongrass and whisk in sweet chili sauce. Transfer into a glass container and let cool. Cover and refrigerate.

For the sweet soy sauce, in a small saucepan over medium heat, warm sugar until it begins to caramelize, stirring constantly, until it turns golden brown. Deglaze with sake, add soy sauce and simmer for 2 minutes. Remove from heat and transfer into a glass container. Let cool. Cover and refrigerate.

To make Japanese rice:

In a rice cooker: Wash rice with cold water, several times, until the water becomes almost clear. Drain rice in a colander and set aside for 30 minutes.

Place rice in rice cooker, add water and let soak for 1 hour. Start cooker and follow manufacturer directions.

In a pot: Wash rice with cold water, several times, until the water becomes almost clear. Drain rice in a colander and set aside for 30 minutes.

Place rice in a small stockpot, add water and let soak for 1 hour. Cover and bring to a boil. Simmer for 20 minutes or until water is almost gone. Remove from heat and let sit for 5 minutes.

Warm hot rocks per manufacturer's directions.

Arrange beef and vegetables on individual platters and serve with dipping sauces and a side dish of rice.

Serves 6.

Difficulty 1.

WINE PAIRING ❧ PINOT NOIR, ESTANCIA, "PINNACLES RANCHES", MONTEREY, CALIFORNIA

Izumi

Doryaki Sandwiches with Green Tea Ice Cream

GREEN TEA ICE CREAM

3 tablespoons (45 ml) hot water
1 tablespoon (15 g) green tea powder
3 egg yolks
1/3 cup (85 g) powdered sugar
1 cup (240 ml) whole milk
1 cup (240 ml) heavy cream, whipped

PANCAKES

4 eggs
2/3 cup (140 g) sugar
3 tablespoons (45 ml) honey
1 tablespoon (15 ml) sake
1 cup (235 g) all-purpose flour
1 teaspoon (5 g) baking powder
2 tablespoons (30 ml) water

FILLING

1 can Ogura-An,
sweetened red bean paste, purchased
1/4 cup (60 ml) whipped cream

GARNISH

1/4 cup (60 g) powdered sugar

EQUIPMENT

2 glass bowls
Chef's knives and cutting board
Glass cup
Griddle or non-stick frying pan
Ice cream maker (optional)
Paper towels
Plastic wrap
Saucepan
Spatula
Wire whisk

To make green tea ice cream, mix hot water and green tea powder in a small glass cup and set aside.

Lightly whisk egg yolks in a saucepan. Add sugar to the pan and mix well. Gradually stir in milk. Place pan on low heat and heat the mixture, stirring constantly. When the mixture has thickened, remove saucepan from the heat.

Soak the bottom of the saucepan in ice water to cool the mixture. Add green tea to egg mixture and mix well, continuing to cool it in ice water. Add whipped heavy cream and stir gently.

Pour mixture into an ice cream maker and freeze, according to manufacturer's instructions.

If you do not have an ice cream maker, pour mixture into a container and freeze, stirring the ice cream a few times.

For pancakes, place eggs, sugar, honey and sake in a large glass or stainless steel bowl and beat with a wire whisk for 4 to 5 minutes or until batter is light and fluffy. Fold in flour and baking powder and mix well. Cover and refrigerate for 15 minutes.

Just before cooking, add water a little at a time to achieve a consistency that is slightly thicker than the batter for breakfast pancakes.

Heat a griddle or non-stick frying pan over medium heat. Grease griddle with an oiled paper towel. Drop a ladleful of batter to create a 3-inch (7.6 cm) diameter pancake.

When the surface of the pancake starts to bubble, flip over and cook the other side for 2 minutes. Transfer pancakes to a platter and keep covered with a moist paper towel to keep them from drying out.

Mix half of the red bean paste with whipped cream.

To make doryaki sandwiches, spread red bean paste or creamy red bean paste on a pancake, ensuring that there is slightly more paste in the center of the pancake so that the finished sandwich's shape will be slightly curved in the middle. Cover with a second pancake and wrap in plastic wrap until ready to eat.

Cut doryakis in half and place on dessert plates. Dust with powdered sugar and serve with a scoop of green tea ice cream.

Serves 6.

Difficulty 2.

Izumi

DINING AT 150 CENTRAL PARK OOZES SOPHISTICATION AND STYLE. THE FINE BONE CHINA COMMISSIONED FROM Raynaud OF Limoges, THE AMAZINGLY DESIGNED Art Nouveau-style MENUS, IMPECCABLE SERVICE, ELEGANTLY DECORATED TABLES AND INCREDIBLE FOOD COME TOGETHER WITH THE PROMISE OF AN UNFORGETTABLE EXPERIENCE.

150 Central Park HAS AN IMPRESSIVE, CONTEMPORARY MULTI-COURSE MENU THAT CHANGES SEASONALLY. THIS TASTING-STYLE MENU IS CREATED WITH DISTINCTIVE INGREDIENTS AND PRESENTED WITH UNIQUELY SHAPED SPOONS AND SMALL PLATES ON PLATTERS OF BONE CHINA AND GLASS TO CREATE AN EXPERIENCE LIKE NO OTHER.

A SPECIAL FEATURE EXCLUSIVE TO 150 CENTRAL PARK IS THE WIDE ARRAY OF IMPORTED SEA SALTS. EACH HAS A UNIQUE COLOR AND FLAVOR THAT ENHANCES THE FOOD AND ELEVATES IT TO UNEXPECTED HEIGHTS.

ADD A MOST EXCLUSIVE WINE LIST, ALONG WITH UNIQUE FRUIT-INFUSED WATERS TO ENHANCE THE UNIQUELY PERFECT DINING EXPERIENCE, AND VOILA!

150 Central Park

"BLT" Salad

PICKLED TOMATOES

1/4 cup (60 g) granulated sugar
1/2 cup (160 ml) water
1/4 cup (60 ml) white wine vinegar
1/4 cup (60 ml) apple cider vinegar
1/2 cinnamon stick
1 bay leaf
1 clove garlic, peeled
1/2 teaspoon (2.5 g) red chili flakes
5 allspice berries
1 1/2 teaspoons (7.5 g) mustard seeds
1 sprig thyme
1/2 teaspoon (2.5 g) coriander seeds

1 cup (115 g) cherry or grape tomatoes
1/2 cup (120 ml) vegetable oil
2 tablespoons (30 ml) extra virgin olive oil
Sea salt

PANCETTA

1/4 cup (60 ml) honey
1/4 cup (60 ml) apple juice
2 tablespoons (30 ml) apple cider vinegar
1 tablespoon (15 g) Dijon mustard
Dash cayenne pepper
4 ounces (120 g) thinly sliced pancetta

QUAIL EGGS

6 quail eggs
1 teaspoon (5 ml) white wine vinegar

ROB ROY VINAIGRETTE

1/2 cup (120 ml) Scotch
3 tablespoons (45 ml) sweet vermouth
3 maraschino cherries
1/2 tablespoon (7.5 g) Dijon mustard
2 tablespoons (30 ml) apple cider vinegar
1/3 cup (90 ml) vegetable oil

AIOLI

2 egg yolks
1 tablespoon (15 ml) white wine vinegar
1 tablespoon (15 g) Dijon mustard
1 cup (240 ml) vegetable oil
1 bunch green onions, washed, trimmed, lightly grilled and coarsely chopped
Salt and freshly ground black pepper

SALAD

3 heads little Gem lettuce or Boston lettuce, washed and trimmed

GARNISH

1 brioche, thinly sliced and toasted
1 green onion, julienned and reserved in ice water

EQUIPMENT

2 cookie sheets
4 saucepans
5 glass bowls
Blender
Chef's knives and cutting board
Fine sieve
Food processor
Metal tongs
Paper towels
Parchment paper
Plastic wrap
Shallow pan
Slotted spoon

Preheat oven to 325°F or 162°C.

To make pickled tomatoes, combine all the ingredients for the pickling liquid in a saucepan and bring to a boil over medium heat. Remove from heat and let cool completely.

Warm oil in a shallow pan over medium-high heat and quickly fry tomatoes in hot oil. Remove tomatoes from oil with a slotted spoon as soon as the skin starts to peel off. Place on a cookie sheet lined with paper towels and allow to cool.

Gently peel skin off tomatoes and discard skin. Divide tomatoes into two glass bowls. Toss the contents of one with olive oil and season with salt. Strain cooled pickling liquid into the other bowl filled with tomatoes. Cover and refrigerate both.

For pancetta, combine all ingredients except pancetta in a small saucepan and mix well. Bring to a boil over medium heat. Reduce heat and simmer for about 20 minutes or until mixture has obtained a glaze-like consistency.

Lay pancetta on a cookie sheet lined with parchment paper and bake for 6 to 8 minutes or until pancetta has rendered most of its fat. Remove from the oven and brush with honey glaze. Return to the oven for 5 minutes to allow the glaze to bake. Remove tray again to turn pancetta slices over, brush with glaze and put back in oven for another 5 minutes. Repeat process two more times. Transfer pancetta crisps to a clean cookie sheet lined with parchment paper and let dry for 2 hours.

Cook quail eggs in boiling water for 2 minutes. Remove from heat and transfer eggs to a glass bowl filled with iced water and white wine vinegar. Carefully peel eggs and place on a small plate. Cover and refrigerate.

For vinaigrette, place Scotch, vermouth and stemmed maraschino cherries in a small saucepan and warm over high heat. Quickly flambé to burn off the alcohol. Reduce heat and simmer for about 20 minutes or until liquid has reduced by half and has a syrupy consistency. Transfer mixture to a blender.

Add mustard and vinegar and blend at high speed, adding half of the vegetable oil a little at a time.

Transfer to a glass bowl and whisk in remaining oil. Set aside.

To make the aioli, place the egg yolks, vinegar and mustard in a food processor and blend. Slowly incorporate oil with the food processor running at medium speed. Add chopped green onions and blend until well combined, but not entirely smooth. Season with salt and pepper. Set aside.

Place a few leaves of lettuce on a chilled plate in a semicircle. Garnish with pickled tomatoes, halved quail eggs and pieces of pancetta. Drizzle with Rob Roy vinaigrette. Finish with a couple pieces of toasted brioche, a few drops of aioli and a sprinkle of julienned green onion.

Serves 6.

Difficulty 3.

WINE PAIRING ☙ MOËT & CHANDON, BRUT, CHAMPAGNE, "IMPÉRIAL", FRANCE

150 Central Park

Camembert and Lager Soup

SOUP

2 tablespoons (30 g) unsalted butter
1 leek, washed, halved lengthwise and sliced
1 parsnip, peeled and chopped
1/2 cup (115 g) celeriac, peeled and chopped
1 clove garlic, peeled and smashed
1 cup (240 ml) whole milk
1 cup (240 ml) vegetable stock (page 156)
1/2 cup (120 ml) heavy cream
1 cup (240 ml) Lager beer, such as Heineken
1 bay leaf
1 tablespoon (15 ml) Worcestershire sauce
1/2 teaspoon (2.5 g) dry mustard
1/2 pound (250 g) camembert cheese,
rind removed and cubed

SPICED POPCORN

1/4 teaspoon (1 ml) vegetable oil
1 cup (60 g) popped corn
2 tablespoons (30 g) granulated sugar
1 tablespoon (15 ml) light corn syrup
1 teaspoon (5 g) unsalted butter
1 teaspoon (5 ml) water
Dash cayenne pepper
Dash ground allspice
Dash freshly ground black pepper
Dash salt

GARNISH

1/4 pound (125 g) thick bacon, cubed
1 ounce (30 g) micro arugula

EQUIPMENT

Blender
Chef's knives and cutting board
Cookie sheet or Silpat
Fine sieve
Ladle
Large glass bowl
Paper towels
Parchment paper
Slotted spoon
Small saucepan
Small sauté pan
Stockpot
Whisk
Wooden spoon

Melt butter in a stockpot over medium heat. Add leek, parsnip, celeriac and garlic and sweat for 5 to 6 minutes or until leek is tender to the touch. Do not brown.

Whisk in milk, vegetable stock, heavy cream and beer. Add bay leaf.

Bring to a boil, then reduce heat to a simmer.

Cook soup for 18 to 20 minutes or until vegetables are cooked throughout, stirring occasionally.

Stir in Worcestershire sauce and dry mustard. Season to taste.

Discard bay leaf. Transfer soup to a blender and blend until smooth. Strain through a fine sieve into a clean pot.

Bring soup back to a simmer over medium heat and whisk in camembert cheese, a handful of cubes at a time. Stirring constantly, simmer until cheese has completely melted. Do not boil.

To make spiced popcorn, place popped corn in a large oiled glass bowl.

Combine sugar, corn syrup, butter and water in a small saucepan and cook over medium heat until mixture reaches 295°F or 146°C. Stir in spices and salt.

Drizzle over popcorn, mixing well using an oiled spoon. Spread on a cookie sheet lined with parchment paper or on a Silpat. Let cool then break into pieces.

For bacon garnish, warm a sauté pan over medium-high heat and sauté bacon cubes for 6 to 8 minutes or until bacon is crispy. Remove bacon from the pan with a slotted spoon onto a plate lined with a paper towel.

Ladle soup into warmed bowls. Garnish with spiced popcorn, cubed bacon and micro arugula.

Serves 6.

Difficulty 2.

150 Central Park Martini

1 1/2 oz. (4.5 cl) GREY GOOSE® Vodka
1/4 oz. (0.75 cl) lemon juice
1/4 oz. (0.75 cl) Monin Lemongrass syrup
3 slices of cucumber
3 basil leaves

Fill shaker with ice and add all ingredients. Shake well and strain into a chilled martini glass. Garnish with a basil leaf.

150 Central Park

Cacio e Pepe Rigatoni

VEGETABLES
1 bunch green asparagus spears, trimmed
5 ounces (140 g) baby spinach

PURÉE
1/2 cup (120 ml) heavy cream
1 shallot, peeled and diced
1 clove garlic, peeled and smashed

PARMESAN BUBBLES
1 cup (240 ml) whole milk
1 3-ounce (85 g) Parmesan rind
1 teaspoon (5 ml) liquid lecithin

MUSHROOMS
1 tablespoon (15 ml) vegetable oil
1 1/2 cups (350 g) hen-of-the-woods (maitake) mushrooms
1 teaspoon (5 g) diced preserved lemon, purchased
Salt and freshly ground black pepper

PASTA
1 pound (450 g) dry rigatoni pasta
Sea salt
1 cup (240 ml) crème fraîche

GARNISH
3 tablespoons (45 g) toasted pine nuts
Chervil leaves
1/4 bunch chives, half chopped and half julienned

EQUIPMENT
3 small saucepans
Blender
Chef's knives and cutting board
Chinois or fine-meshed strainer
Large sauté pan
Sieve
Spatula
Stockpot

Cut the tips off the asparagus spears and blanch. Set aside.

Cut the rest of the spears in half cross-wise. Take the top halves and slice into small coin-like disks. Blanch and set aside.

Blanch bottom halves of the asparagus spears and spinach. Drain and set aside.

Place heavy cream, shallot and garlic in a small saucepan and bring to a simmer over medium heat.

Cook for 10 to 12 minutes or until cream is fragrant and slightly thick.

Strain cream through a sieve into a clean small saucepan.

Place blanched spinach and asparagus half-spears in a blender. Add garlic-infused cream and blend until smooth. Pass through a chinois or fine-mesh strainer, forcing the purée through the holes with a spatula. Keep warm.

To make Parmesan bubbles, place milk and Parmesan in a small saucepan and infuse over low heat for 30 minutes. Remove Parmesan rind and discard. Keep warm.

Sauté mushrooms in hot oil over medium-high heat for 5 minutes. Add preserved lemon, blanched asparagus tips and disks and cook for 2 minutes or until heated throughout. Season with salt and pepper.

Cook rigatoni pasta in a stockpot of boiling salted water until al dente, about 12 minutes. Drain well and toss with crème fraîche in a large sauté pan. Cook until crème fraîche has thickened and coats pasta thoroughly.

Place warm Parmesan-infused milk into the blender. Add lecithin and blend until the milk separates and makes foam.

To serve, place a spoonful of the spinach asparagus cream purée into warm pasta bowls.

Top with rigatoni pasta and garnish with mushrooms and asparagus. Garnish with a dollop of Parmesan foam and sprinkle with toasted pine nuts and fresh herbs.

Serves 6.

Difficulty 1.

Cucumber Cocktail

2 thin cucumber slices, skin on
1 oz. (3 cl) fresh lime juice
2 oz. (6 cl) gin
1 oz. (3 cl) simple syrup (page 157)

Combine cucumber and lime juice in a mixing glass. Using a muddler, mash cucumber until broken into small pieces. Add gin and simple syrup and transfer into an ice filled cocktail shaker. Shake well, pour into rock glass and garnish with a cucumber wheel.

WINE PAIRING ∽ BOTTEGA VINAIA, PINO GRIGIO, TRENTINO, ITALY

150 Central Park

WINE PAIRING ❦ TREANA, VIOGNIER/MARSANNE, "MER SOLEIL VINEYARD", CENTRAL COAST, CALIFORNIA

Corn Nut Crusted Halibut

SIMPLE SYRUP

1/4 cup (60 g) granulated sugar
1/3 cup (90 ml) water

MARINADE

1/3 cup (90 ml) water
1/4 cup (60 g) kosher salt
2 tablespoons (30 g) granulated sugar
1 lemon, cut into wedges
2 thyme sprigs
6 black peppercorns
6 coriander seeds

FISH

1 1/2 pounds (700 g) halibut, trimmed into
6 diamond shapes, about 4 ounces each
1/4 cup (60 g) corn nuts
1/4 cup (60 g) corn meal
1 tablespoon (15 g) dry ranch
seasoning blend, purchased
1 egg, beaten
3 tablespoons (45 ml) vegetable oil

HOLLANDAISE

1 pound (450 g) unsalted butter
1 shallot, peeled and sliced
5 black peppercorns
2 stems parsley
2 tablespoons (30 ml) white wine vinegar
1 tablespoon (15 ml) water
4 egg yolks
Juice of 1/2 freshly squeezed lemon
1 teaspoon (5 g) dry ranch seasoning blend
Salt

CABBAGE SLAW

1/2 cup (115 g) minced red cabbage
1 fennel bulb, minced
2 carrots, peeled and minced
1/2 small red onion, peeled and minced
1/4 teaspoon (1.2 g) celery seeds
1 teaspoon (56 g) Dijon mustard
3 tablespoons (45 ml) rice wine vinegar
1 egg yolk
1/2 cup (120 ml) vegetable oil
1 teaspoon (5 ml) Sriracha
hot chili sauce, purchased

SORREL PUDDING

2 shallots, peeled and diced
1/2 cup (120 ml) heavy cream
5 ounces (140 g) baby spinach, blanched
1 bunch sorrel, trimmed

VEGETABLES

3 carrots, peeled, turned and blanched
3 stalks celery, peeled, cut into diamonds and
blanched
6 baby turnips, halved and blanched
3/4 cup (180 ml) vegetable stock (page 156)
1/4 cup (60 ml) simple syrup
1 tablespoon (15 g) unsalted butter

POMMES PONT NEUF

1/2 cup (120 ml) vegetable oil
1 clove garlic, peeled and smashed
2 fresh thyme sprigs
2 large Yukon Gold potatoes,
peeled and cut in 2-inch batons

GARNISH

2 multi-colored carrots, peeled,
shaved and soaked in iced water
2 radishes, shaved and soaked in iced water

EQUIPMENT

2 medium glass bowls
2 small saucepans
3 saucepans
Baking dish
Blender
Chef's knives and cutting board
Double boiler
Food processor
Frying pan
Glass bowl
Large sauté pan
Ovenproof baking dish
Paper towels
Parchment paper
Plastic wrap
Sieve
Slotted spoon
Small cookie sheet
Small glass bowl
Spatula
Whisk

Preheat oven to 320°F or 160°C.

Prepare syrup by mixing all ingredients in a small saucepan and boiling until sugar has melted. Let cool.

To make marinade, place all ingredients in a saucepan and bring to a boil over medium heat. Remove from heat and let cool. Strain liquid over a glass bowl. Cover and refrigerate for 30 minutes.

Place cut halibut in a baking dish and cover with marinade. Cover with plastic wrap and refrigerate for 15 minutes. Grind corn nuts in a food processor and force through a sieve with a spatula. Discard pieces that do not pass through it.

Combine ground corn nuts and corn meal in a glass bowl. Season with dry ranch seasoning and mix well.

Remove fish from baking dish and discard marinade. Rinse fish pieces and pat dry using paper towels. Dip each piece into the egg mixture to coat it, then dredge in the corn mixture. Place on a small cookie sheet and set aside.

For hollandaise, slowly melt butter in a small saucepan over medium heat.

Combine shallots, peppercorns, white wine vinegar and parsley stems in a small saucepan and bring to a simmer over medium heat. Simmer for 10 minutes or until all liquid has been absorbed. Add water. Strain through a sieve into a medium-sized glass bowl and whisk in egg yolks. Place the bowl over a double boiler of simmering water, ensuring that there is no direct contact between the bowl and the water. Whisk in butter 1 tablespoon (15 g) at a time until all the butter has been incorporated. Add lemon juice, ranch seasoning and salt and mix well. Remove from heat, cover and keep on the side of the stove.

To make slaw, combine cabbage, fennel, carrots and onion in a bowl and toss with celery seeds.

Place egg, mustard and rice vinegar in a blender and blend together. With blender running at medium speed, add oil and Sriracha chili sauce in a slow drizzle. Add dressing to cabbage and toss well.

For sorrel pudding, combine cream and shallots in a saucepan and bring to a boil over medium heat.

Place sorrel and blanched spinach in a blender. Strain shallot from cream and add to spinach. Blend until smooth, adding cream in small amounts to obtain a thick pudding-like consistency. Transfer to a small glass bowl and set aside.

Heat oil in a large sauté pan over medium-high heat and sear fish on each side for 2 minutes. Transfer to an ovenproof baking dish and bake for 5 minutes.

Finish vegetables by placing the carrots, celery and turnips in a saucepan filled with the vegetable stock, syrup and butter. Cover with a piece of parchment paper. Bring to a simmer over medium-high heat and cook for 5 to 7 minutes or until vegetables are soft to the touch.

For pommes pont neuf, heat oil in a frying pan over medium-high heat. Add garlic, thyme and potatoes and fry for 8 to 10 minutes, stirring occasionally so potatoes do not stick together.

Remove potatoes from hot oil with a slotted spoon and place on a platter lined with paper towels. Discard garlic and thyme. Season with salt.

To serve, use a soup spoon to place several spoonfuls of hollandaise in the center of a warm plate. Top sauce with piece of halibut. Place a dumpling (rounded spoonful) of cabbage slaw askew on the fish. Arrange vegetables and potatoes in a line on each side of the fish with dollops of sorrel pudding. Garnish with micro sorrel.

Serves 6.

Difficulty 4.

150 Central Park

Root Beer Glazed Duck Breast

DUCK

2 teaspoons (10 g) sassafras (gumbo file powder)
1/2 teaspoon (2.5 g) star anise, toasted
1/2 teaspoon (2.5 g) fennel seeds, toasted
1/2 teaspoon (2.5 g) black peppercorns, toasted
1/2 teaspoon (2.5 g) juniper berries
1/4 vanilla pod, seeds only, pod reserved
1/4 cup (60 g) salt
2 tablespoons (30 g) granulated sugar
6 7.5-ounce (212 g) duck breasts
2 bottles root beer
1 tablespoon (15 g) fennel seeds, toasted
2 tablespoons (30 g) molasses
2 black peppercorns, toasted
2 bay leaves
1/2 stick cinnamon
Reserved vanilla pod
1 tablespoon (15 ml) sherry vinegar
1/3 cup (90 ml) demi-glace (page 157)

SMOKED SWEET POTATOES

2 sweet potatoes, peeled and cubed
1/4 cup (60 ml) heavy cream
1 tablespoon (15 g) butter
1 teaspoon (5 g) brown sugar

DATES

12 dates
1/4 cup (60 g) granulated sugar
1/4 cup (60 ml) water
1/4 cup (60 ml) white wine
1/2 cup (120 ml) white wine vinegar
1/2 stick of cinnamon
1 allspice berry
1 clove
2 black peppercorns
2 juniper berries
2 strips orange zest
1/4 teaspoon (1.2 g) sassafras (gumbo file powder)

VEGETABLES

12 baby turnips, peeled and halved
12 Brussels sprouts, trimmed and halved
1/2 cup (120 ml) vegetable stock (page 156)
1 tablespoon (15 g) salted butter
Salt

EQUIPMENT

3 small saucepans
Aluminum foil
Baking dish
Blender
Carving knife, Chef's knives and cutting board
Colander
Food processor
Grilling tray
Hotel pan
Large sauté pan
Lid
Medium saucepan
Paper towels
Pastry brush
Pot
Sauté pan
Sieve
Small glass bowl
Small pot
Whisk
Wire rack

Preheat oven to 135°F or 57°C.

For duck, place sassafras, star anise, fennel seeds, peppercorn and juniper berries in a food processor and grind until fine.

Mix spices with vanilla seeds, salt and sugar in a small bowl. Rub into duck breasts. Arrange in a baking dish. Cover and refrigerate overnight.

Thoroughly rinse duck breasts and pat dry with paper towels. Score duck fat with a sharp knife. Warm a large sauté pan over medium heat and place duck breasts, skin side down in the pan. Sauté for 5 to 7 minutes to render the fat.

Transfer onto a wire rack placed inside an ovenproof baking dish. Cover with aluminum foil, then with a lid. Bake in the oven for 45 minutes. Once cooked, remove from oven and let sit for 10 minutes.

While the duck is cooking, place root beer, fennel seeds, molasses, peppercorn, bay leaves, cinnamon and vanilla pod in a small saucepan over medium heat. Simmer for 18 to 20 minutes or until mixture reaches the consistency of a glaze. Stir in sherry vinegar and set aside. Strain just before using.

Prepare grill for smoking as per manufacturer's instructions and preheat to 350°F or 176°C.

Place potatoes onto a grilling tray positioned on the far side of the grate, away from the fire. Close the lid on the grill; smoke potatoes for 20 minutes.

Transfer sweet potatoes to a pot and cover with cold water. Bring to a boil and cook for 20 minutes. Drain using a colander.

Heat cream and butter in a small saucepan over medium heat.

Transfer potatoes to a blender and blend until smooth, adding cream mixture a little at a time. Add brown sugar and pulse blender one more time. Scoop mashed sweet potatoes into a small pot. Season with salt. Cover and keep on the side of the stove.

To make the dates, place all the ingredients in a saucepan and bring to a simmer over medium heat. Cook for 15 minutes or until dates are plumped and tender. Strain the liquid and reserve.

Peel skin off the dates and place back into the liquid. Discard the spices, peels and skins.

Brush duck breast skin with root beer glaze.

Transfer breasts to a carving surface or cutting board and trim to a rectangular shape.

Remove dates from liquid and pat dry.

Braise turnips and Brussels sprouts in vegetable stock for 8 to 10 minutes or until vegetables are soft to the touch.

Drain and sauté Brussels sprouts in melted butter in a small sauté pan over medium-high heat. Season with salt.

Warm demi-glace in a small saucepan over medium heat. Whisk in root beer glaze a little at a time, tasting often until sauce is slightly sweet.

Arrange one portion of duck breast in the center of a warm plate. Add sweet potato purée, in the form of tear drops, on both sides of the duck. Position the dates, turnips and Brussels sprouts around the duck. Serve with the root beer demi-glace sauce.

Serves 6.

Difficulty 4.

WINE PAIRING ❧ LOUIS JADOT, CHARDONNAY, MEURSAULT, FRANCE

150 Central Park

WINE PAIRING ✍ CHAMPAGNE BARONS DE ROTHSCHILD, BRUT, CHAMPAGNE, FRANCE

Sticky Toffee Pudding

FROZEN YOGURT
2 cups (465 g) Greek yogurt
2/3 cup (160 g) granulated sugar
1 teaspoon (5 ml) vanilla extract
1/2 teaspoon (2.5 ml) lemon extract

ENGLISH PUDDING
3/4 pound (375 g) dates, pitted
3 cups (720 ml) boiling water
1 teaspoon (5 g) baking soda
2 cups (465 g) unsalted butter, room temperature
3 cups (700 g) confectioner's sugar
3 eggs
2 1/4 cups (525 g) all-purpose flour
1 teaspoon (5 g) ground cinnamon
1/2 teaspoon (2.5 g) ground star anise
1/4 teaspoon (1 g) ground allspice
1/4 teaspoon (1 g) ground cloves

CARAMEL SAUCE
1 cup (240 g) sugar
2 tablespoons (30 ml) honey
3 tablespoons (45 ml) water
1 cup (240 ml) heavy cream
1/2 teaspoon (2.5 ml) vanilla extract

GARNISH
4 vanilla wafers, ground
4 chocolate wafers, ground
1 tablespoon (15 g) cocoa powder
1 pack white cotton candy, purchased

EQUIPMENT
2 large bowls
9-inch (23 cm) round cake pan
Blender
Cookie cutter
Handheld mixer
Ice cream maker (optional)
Paring knife
Small bowl
Small saucepan
Wire rack
Wooden spoon

Preheat oven to 356°F or 180°C.

Grease cake pan and dust with a little flour.

To make frozen yogurt, mix all the ingredients together in a large glass bowl. Stir until sugar has completely dissolved.

Pour mixture into an ice cream maker and freeze, according to manufacturer's instructions.

If you do not have an ice cream maker, pour mixture into a container and freeze, stirring the ice cream a few times.

To make cake for pudding, put dates, water and baking soda in a blender and blend until smooth.

Place butter and sugar in a large glass bowl and beat with a handheld mixer at medium speed until mixture is soft and creamy. Reduce speed to low and add eggs one at a time. Fold in flour, followed by date purée and spices.

Spoon batter in cake pan. Place cake pan into a deeper baking pan. Pour hot water into the baking pan until the water level is one inch from the top of the cake pan. Bake for 35 to 40 minutes or until a toothpick inserted in the center of the cake comes out clean.

Once cooked, remove cake from the baking pan and let cool on a wire rack for 30 minutes.

To make caramel sauce, melt sugar and water in a small saucepan over low heat. Add honey. Increase heat and boil for 5 minutes or until mixture turns a golden shade.

Remove from heat. Stand back to avoid burning before gradually stirring in heavy cream and vanilla extract. Simmer, stirring constantly, for 2 to 3 minutes or until caramel sauce is smooth and thick.

Remove from heat and let cool.

Cut cake into disc shapes using a round cookie cutter.

Mix wafers in a small bowl.

Dust half of a dessert plate with cocoa powder. Arrange a small circle of wafer mix on one side of the plate and top with a rounded spoonful of frozen yogurt. Place toffee pudding cake next to the yogurt and top with a spoonful of caramel sauce and a piece of cotton candy.

Serves 6.

Difficulty 3.

Caramel Coffee

1/2 oz. (1.5 cl) Monin caramel syrup
Piping hot coffee
Whipped cream

Pour caramel syrup in an Irish coffee mug. Fill with coffee and top with a rosette of whipped cream.

150 Central Park

An Italian Trattoria with both indoor and al fresco seating featuring Italian classics served family style.

Architectural influences from the landscapes of Tuscany come together to create an atmosphere of casual, relaxed elegance. Vaulted ceilings and alcoves with flickering candles, Italian-style paintings purchased in flea markets combined with street vendors and small vintage shops straight out of France and England, enhanced by fresh herbs on the window sill and the subtle aroma of freshly roasted garlic are the trademarks here at Giovanni's.

Giovanni's Tuscan-inspired menu reflects the flavors of the region as well. From the Foccaccia per Due, freshly sliced prosciutto and Ferrari "affettatrice" (a traditional hand-cranked meat slicer), to the hard Italian cheeses, herbal breads and iced Limoncello, you'll think you were dining along the Amalfi coast.

Combine a plate of Lasagna, seasoned by your waiter with a personalized, one-of-a kind pepper grinder, together with some decadent desserts and Giovani's will bring out the Italian in you. Buonissimo!

Giovanni's Table

Mozzarella in Carrozza alla Giovanni

(Wrapped Mozzarella Giovanni Style)

MOZZARELLA CROSTINI
*2 loaves of ciabatta bread
or French baguette, purchased
3 spheres of mozzarella di buffalo,
cut into 1/2-inch (1.2 cm) thick slices
12 thin slices of prosciutto, purchased*

DIJON DRESSING
*1 tablespoon (15 g) Dijon mustard
Juice of 1/2 freshly squeezed lemon
1 teaspoon (5 g) granulated sugar or honey
1/3 cup (90 ml) extra virgin olive oil
Salt
Freshly ground black pepper*

SALAD
*1 bulb fennel, shaved and kept in ice water
6 ounces (170 g) mâche (lamb's lettuce)
4 ounces (120 g) arugula
1/2 head radicchio, julienned
2 ounces (60 g) assorted micro greens*

EQUIPMENT
*Blender
Chef's knives and cutting board
Cookie sheet
Glass bowl
Parchment paper*

Preheat oven to 333°F or 165°C.

Cut ciabatta loaves in 1/4-inch (1 cm) thick slices, using only the center slices for length, and place on a cookie sheet lined with parchment paper. Drizzle each slice with olive oil.

Wrap mozzarella slices with prosciutto and place two wrapped pieces atop each ciabatta slice. Bake for 4 to 5 minutes or until mozzarella starts to melt and prosciutto gets crispy.

While mozzarella is baking, place all the ingredients for the dressing in a blender. Season to taste with salt and pepper and blend until smooth and emulsified.

For salad, drain fennel and place with all the salad varieties in a glass bowl. Mix well and arrange on chilled appetizer plates.

Place one mozzarella crostini on each plate, next to the salad. Finish with a drizzle of Dijon dressing.

Serves 6.

Difficulty 1.

Bellini

*1 fresh peach, peeled, pitted and quartered
or 1/4 cup frozen peaches, thawed
1/4 teaspoon (1 g) grated orange zest
2 oz. (6 cl) simple syrup (page 157)
3 oz. (9 cl) Prosecco or sparkling wine*

Place first 3 ingredients in a blender and purée until smooth. Pour 2 tablespoons of peach mixture into a Champagne flute and slowly top off with Prosecco. Stir to blend and garnish with a peach sliver.

WINE PAIRING ⟁ ALBOLA, PINOT GRIGIO, FRIULI, ITALY

Giovanni's Table

WINE PAIRING ❧ FEUDI DI SAN GREGORIO, FALANGHINA, SANNIO, ITALY

Sformato di Fontina e Spinaci con Funghi Trifolati e Pomodorini (Double-baked Fontina and Spinach Soufflé)

ONION CONFIT
2 medium onions, peeled and shaved
1/3 cup (90 ml) extra virgin olive oil

SOUFFLÉS
1/2 cup (115 g) unsalted butter
1/2 cup (115 g) all-purpose flour
2 1/2 cups (600 ml) warm milk
1/4 cup (60 g) grated Parmesan cheese
3/4 cup (175 g) shredded Fontina cheese
1 tablespoon (15 g) Dijon mustard
5 eggs, yolk and white separated
4 ounces (120 g) baby spinach, blanched, water squeezed out and chopped
Salt and freshly ground white pepper

PARMESAN GLAZE
1/2 cup (120 ml) heavy cream
1/4 cup (60 g) grated Parmesan cheese
Salt and freshly ground white pepper

VEGETABLE RAGOÛT
1 tablespoon (15 ml) extra virgin olive oil
2 cloves garlic, peeled and chopped
4 ounces (120 g) button mushrooms, quartered
1/4 cup (60 ml) dry white wine
1/2 cup (115 g) cherry tomatoes, halved lengthwise
Salt and freshly ground black pepper
1 tablespoon (15 g) chopped parsley

GARNISH
Chive sprigs

EQUIPMENT
9" x 13" (23 x 33 cm) or larger glass or ovenproof baking dish
2 wire whisks
3 saucepans
6 ramekins or soufflé cups
Chef's knife and cutting board
Large glass or stainless steel bowl
Medium sauté pan
Stand mixer with whisk attachment or large copper or stainless steel mixer
Wooden spoon

Preheat oven to 300°F or 150°C.

For confit, in a small saucepan over medium heat, simmer onion in olive oil for 20 minutes. Do not brown. Allow to cool. Cover and reserve.

To make soufflés, in a small saucepan over low heat, melt butter and whisk in flour. Cook roux for 2 minutes (do not brown) then slowly incorporate milk, stirring constantly for 5 to 6 minutes or until smooth and thickened. Remove from heat and allow to cool slightly.

Stir in Parmesan and Fontina cheese. Add Dijon mustard and egg yolks, one at a time, mixing thoroughly. At last fold in chopped spinach and season with salt and pepper.

In a mixing bowl, beat egg whites and a pinch of salt with an electric mixer on medium speed until eggs are frothy. Increase speed to high and beat until they form soft peaks.

Spoon 1/3 of egg whites in cheese mixture and gently mix until the batter is lightened. Fold in remaining egg whites, taking care not to deflate them. Divide mixture into greased individual molds set in a shallow pan or baking dish. Pour water into the pan until it is halfway up the sides of the molds and bake for 20 to 25 minutes or until soufflés have risen and are lightly colored. Remove from heat and allow cooling.

In a small saucepan over medium heat, bring heavy cream to a boil. Remove from heat and whisk in cheese. Season to taste and keep warm.

For ragoût, in a sauté pan over medium heat, warm oil and sauté garlic for 2 minutes. Add mushrooms and sauté for 2 to 3 minutes. Deglaze with wine and add tomatoes. Season with salt and pepper and simmer until all liquid has evaporated. Stir in parsley at the last minute.

Just before serving, remove soufflés from molds and reheat for 5 to 7 minutes or until the soufflés rise again. Delicately center each soufflé on a warmed plate. Coat with Parmesan glaze and surround with vegetable ragoût. Garnish with chive sprigs.

Serves 6.

Difficulty 4.

Giovanni's Table

Insalata alla Cesare (Caesar Salad)

CROUTONS
1 cup (250 g) cubed sourdough bread
4 tablespoons (60 ml) extra virgin olive oil
Salt and freshly ground black pepper

DRESSING
3 cloves garlic
3 tablespoons (45 ml) freshly squeezed
lemon juice
5 anchovy fillets, drained or
2 teaspoons (10 g) anchovy paste
2 teaspoons (10 g) Dijon mustard
2 teaspoons (10 ml) Worcestershire sauce
2 egg yolks
1 cup (240 ml) extra virgin olive oil
Salt

INGREDIENTS
3/4 pound (375 g) radicchio, sliced
3/4 pound (375 g) romaine, sliced
1/4 cup (60 g) Parmesan cheese, shaved

EQUIPMENT
Blender or food processor
Chef's knife and cutting board
Paper towels
Small glass or stainless steel bowl
Standard baking sheet

Preheat oven to 380°F or 195°C.

To prepare croutons, place bread on a baking sheet and drizzle with olive oil. Toss well to coat evenly. Season to taste with salt and black pepper. Bake for 10 minutes or until crisp and golden brown. Rotate to ensure even browning. Set aside to cool on a paper towel.

To prepare Caesar dressing, combine all ingredients except oil in a blender or food processor. Blend until smooth. While processing, slowly add oil. Adjust seasoning, transfer in a small glass or stainless steel bowl, cover and refrigerate.

Place radicchio and romaine lettuces on chilled plates, drizzle with Caesar dressing, and garnish with Parmesan shavings and croutons.

Serve immediately.

Serves 6.

Difficulty 1.

Giovanni's Table

WINE PAIRING ⌒ MANDRAROSSA, NERO D' AVOLA, SICILIA, ITALY

Focaccie alla Giovanni (Italian Flat Bread Giovanni's Style)

DOUGH

2 tablespoons (30 g) yeast
1/4 cup (60 ml) hot water
4 cups (920 g) all-purpose flour, sifted
1 tablespoon (15 g) salt
2 tablespoons (30 ml) extra virgin olive oil
1 3/4 cups (420 ml) water, room temperature

1/4 cup (60 ml) extra virgin
olive oil for drizzling

TOMATO SAUCE

2 tablespoons (30 ml) extra virgin olive oil
1 yellow onion, chopped
2 cloves garlic, chopped
1 tablespoon (15 g) tomato paste
2 pounds (900 g) fresh tomatoes,
peeled, seeded and diced
1/2 teaspoon (2.5 g) granulated sugar
Salt and freshly ground black pepper
1/4 bunch fresh basil, julienned

GARNISH

2 cups (465 g) shredded mozzarella cheese
1/4 bunch basil, julienned

EQUIPMENT

12" x 18" (30 cm x 45 cm) baking pan
2 standard baking sheets
4 medium glass or stainless steel bowls
Chef's knife and cutting board
Large glass or stainless steel bowl
Medium saucepan
Pastry rack or cooling rack
Small glass bowl
Wooden spoon

Preheat oven to 420°F or 215°C.

For dough, dissolve yeast and hot water in a small glass bowl. Let sit for 2 minutes or until water is cloudy. Place flour and salt in a large glass or stainless steel bowl. Pour in yeast mixture and remaining ingredients and, using a fork, mix thoroughly until dough forms a ball.

Divide into 4 equal pieces and place each dough into a separate oiled bowl. Cover each bowl with plastic wrap and let rest for 1 hour at room temperature.

Transfer dough into an oiled baking pan and spread very gently with oiled fingers until desired thickness, about 1 1/2-inch or 4 cm thick. Repeat with remaining dough.

Drizzle with olive oil and, using your fingers, gently imprint holes in the dough surface; this increases the surface area of the dough and aids in even baking. Let rest for 1 hour.

Meanwhile, prepare the tomato sauce by warming the oil in a saucepan over medium heat. Add onions and sauté for 5 minutes or until translucent. Add garlic, tomato paste, fresh tomatoes and sugar. Season with salt and pepper, bring to a boil and simmer for 20 minutes or until tomatoes are fully cooked and sauce has thickened. Stir in basil at the last minute.

Drizzle the surface of each dough with more oil, spread with tomato sauce and liberally sprinkle with shredded cheese. Finish with fresh julienned basil.

Bake for 25 minutes and allow to cool for a couple minutes before slicing.

You can customize your bread in many ways – try different toppings such as oregano, sliced tomatoes, sautéed potatoes, Parma ham…

You can also add ingredients to the dough. Once the dry ingredients are incorporated add items such as sliced kalamata olives, fresh herbs, chopped walnuts…

Makes 4 pieces.

Difficulty 2.

Giovanni's Table

Pappardelle alla Crema di Radicchio e Pancetta

(Creamy Radicchio and Pancetta Pappardelle)

SAUCE

1 tablespoon (15 ml) extra virgin olive oil
3 tablespoons (45 g) salted butter
1 yellow onion, peeled and diced
1 shallot, peeled and diced
2 cloves garlic, peeled and chopped
1 pound (450 g) pancetta, julienned
2 heads of radicchio, trimmed, julienned and soaked in cold water overnight
1/4 cup (60 ml) white wine
1/2 cup (120 ml) demi-glace (page 157)
3 tablespoons (45 ml) heavy cream
Salt and freshly ground black pepper

TOMATO SAUCE

1 yellow onion, peeled and diced
2 cloves garlic, peeled and crushed
2 tablespoons (30 ml) extra virgin olive oil
1 20-ounce (570 g) can crushed tomatoes
Sprig fresh thyme
Salt and freshly ground black pepper

1 pound (450 g) dry pappardelle pasta
1 teaspoon (5 ml) extra virgin olive oil

2 tablespoons (30 g) Parmesan cheese, grated

GARNISH

2 tablespoons (30 g) Parmesan cheese, shaved
1/4 bunch parsley, finely chopped
Parsley sprigs

EQUIPMENT

Chef's knives and cutting board
Colander
Heavy saucepan
Large pot or stockpot
Sauté pan
Wooden spoon

In a heavy saucepan over medium heat, warm olive oil and 1 tablespoon (15 g) butter and sauté onions and shallots for 5 minutes or until onions are translucent. Add garlic and sauté for 1 minute; do not brown. Increase heat to medium high and add pancetta. Cook for 7 minutes or until pancetta is well done.

Drain radicchio julienne, add to pan and cook for 3 minutes.

Deglaze with white wine and reduce by half.

Add demi-glace and heavy cream, reduce heat and simmer for 10 minutes.

Season with salt and pepper.

For tomato sauce, sauté onion and garlic in hot olive oil in a sauté pan over medium-high heat. Add crushed tomatoes and bring to a simmer.

Add fresh thyme. Season with salt and pepper and simmer for 15 to 20 minutes or until sauce has reduced by half.

While sauces are simmering, cook pappardelle in a stockpot of boiling, salted water until al dente, about 8 minutes. Drain well and toss with olive oil.

Mix both sauces together. Add pasta to sauce and toss to coat. Fold in Parmesan cheese and serve in warm pasta bowls.

Garnish with shaved Parmesan cheese, chopped parsley and parsley sprigs.

Serves 4.

Difficulty 1.

WINE PAIRING ❧ MICHELE CHIARLO, BARBERA D' ASTI, "LE ORME", SUPERIORE, ITALY

Giovanni's Table

Filetti di Sogliola alla Mugnaia

(Sole Fillets Mugnaia)

BRAISED POTATOES

2 medium yellow onions, peeled and chopped
1/4 cup (60 ml) extra virgin olive oil
2 pounds (900 g) Idaho potatoes,
  peeled and cut into 1-inch (2.5 cm) slices
1 1/2 cups (360 ml) chicken stock (page 156)
1/4 cup (60 g) unsalted butter
Salt and freshly ground black pepper

FISH

12 3-ounce (85 g) sole fillets
1/4 cup (60 g) all-purpose flour
1/4 cup (60 ml) extra virgin olive oil
1/4 cup (60 ml) dry white wine
1/2 cup (120 ml) clam juice
Juice of 2 freshly squeezed lemons
Salt and freshly ground black pepper
2 tablespoons (30 g) freshly chopped parsley

VEGETABLE RIBBONS

2 tablespoons (30 ml) extra virgin olive oil
2 cloves garlic, peeled and chopped
3 zucchini, washed and cut into
  ribbons with a mandolin
3 yellow squash, washed and cut into
  ribbons with a mandolin
1 red bell pepper, washed and cut into
  ribbons with a mandolin
1 tablespoon (15 g) freshly chopped parsley

GARNISH

2 lemons, thinly sliced

EQUIPMENT

2 large sauté pans
Chef's knives and cutting board
Fine sieve
Heavy sauté pan
Kitchen tongs
Ladle
Mandolin
Paper towels
Saucepan
Shallow glass bowl
Wooden spoon

To make braised potatoes, saute onions for 5 minutes in hot oil in a heavy sauté pan over medium heat. Do not brown. Add potatoes and toss well. Slowly incorporate chicken stock one ladleful at a time along with a few pieces of butter, stirring frequently after each addition until liquid is absorbed.

Season with salt and ground pepper.

While potatoes are cooking, pat sole fillets dry with paper towels and season them with salt and pepper. Place flour in a glass bowl. Dredge sole fillets in flour, shaking off the excess.

Warm olive oil in a large sauté pan over medium-high heat and sear sole fillets for 1 minute on each side. Remove from pan and transfer to a platter lined with paper towels.

Deglaze pan with white wine and reduce by half. Add clam juice and lemon juice and bring to a boil. Simmer for 2 to 3 minutes and pass through a fine sieve into a clean saucepan.

Reduce heat and place sole fillets back in the pan. Keep warm. Sprinkle with freshly chopped parsley just before plating.

For vegetables, warm olive oil in a large sauté pan over medium heat and sauté garlic, zucchini, squash and bell peppers for 5 minutes or until vegetables are tender. Season with salt and black pepper and toss with chopped parsley.

Place a mound of braised potatoes in the center of warmed entrée plates and top with sautéed vegetable ribbons. Place sole fillets at an angle on top of the vegetables. Drizzle with wine lemon sauce and garnish with a couple of lemon slices.

Serves 6.

Difficulty 2.

Wild Blossom Martini

1 1/4 oz. (3.75 cl) gin
3/4 oz. (2.25 cl) St. Germain Elderflower liqueur
1/4 oz. (0.75 cl) Amaretto Disaronno Originale
1/4 oz. (0.75 cl) Patrón Citronage orange liqueur
1 oz. (3 cl) Sweet & Sour mix

Combine all ingredients in a cocktail shaker with ice. Shake and strain into a chilled martini glass. Garnish with a lemon twist.

Giovanni's Table

Ossobuco alla Piemontese (Veal Ossobuco Au Jus)

VEAL SHANKS
2 tablespoons (30 ml) extra virgin olive oil
6 12-ounce to 1 pound
(340 to 375 g) veal shank
2 yellow onions, small diced
2 carrots, small diced
2 celery stalks, small diced
2 cloves garlic, peeled and diced
1 cup (240 ml) dry white wine
1 15-ounce (450 g) can diced tomatoes
3 cups (710 ml) demi-glace (page 157)
Salt and freshly ground black pepper

MUSHROOMS
1 tablespoon (15 ml) extra virgin olive oil
1 clove garlic, peeled and minced
5 ounces (140 g) button mushrooms, quartered
3 ounces (85 g) cherry tomatoes, quartered
Salt and freshly ground black pepper

BEANS
2 tablespoons (30 g) butter
8 ounces (230 g) green beans,
blanched and refreshed in ice water
Salt

POLENTA
1 1/2 quarts (1.4 L) water
2 teaspoons (10 g) salt
1 3/4 cups (410 g) yellow cornmeal
3 tablespoons (45 g) butter
1/4 cup (60 g) Parmesan, grated

GARNISH
Rosemary sprigs

EQUIPMENT
Cheesecloth
Chef's knife and cutting board
Heavy pot or Dutch oven
Large saucepan
Large sauté pan
Metal tongs
Small sauté pan
Wooden spoon
Wire whisk

Preheat oven to 375°F or 190°C.

Season veal shanks with salt and pepper. Heat a Dutch oven or heavy stockpot over medium-high heat for 2 minutes. Warm oil and sear veal shanks in batches, turning occasionally, until they are well browned on all sides, about 8 minutes. Remove shanks and set aside.

Into the same Dutch oven, add onions, carrots, celery and garlic and sauté for 5 minutes. Deglaze with wine, add tomatoes and demi-glace and bring to a boil. Return shanks to Dutch oven, making sure that they are covered in liquid. Cover and cook in the oven for 1 1/2 hours, turning occasionally, until meat is falling off the bone.

Remove shanks from pot and keep warm. Strain liquid through a cheesecloth. Skim off all the fat that rises to the surface of the jus. Season with salt and pepper to taste.

In a small sauté pan over medium heat, warm oil and sauté garlic for 2 minutes. Add mushrooms and tomatoes and sauté for 3 minutes. Stir in 1/2 cup (120 ml) of the jus and simmer for 10 minutes or until mushrooms are cooked through. Season with salt and pepper and keep warm.

Simmer the remaining jus for 10 minutes or until it has reduced by half.

Make polenta by bringing a heavy saucepan of salted water to a boil over high heat and gradually whisking in cornmeal. Reduce heat to low and cook, stirring often for about 15 minutes or until mixture thickens and cornmeal is tender. Add butter and Parmesan cheese. Taste and adjust seasoning as needed.

For green beans, in a large sauté pan over medium heat, melt butter and sauté for 3 minutes, or until warm. Season with salt.

Arrange polenta off-center on warmed plates, top with green beans and veal shank. Spoon mushroom mixture around ossobuco and garnish with a rosemary sprig. Finish off with a drizzle of au jus.

Serves 6.

Difficulty 5.

WINE PAIRING ❧ LA VITE, TOSCANA, "LUCENTE", ITALY

Giovanni's Table

WINE PAIRING ☙ RAVENSWOOD, "OLD VINE" ZINFANDEL, SONOMA, CALIFORNIA

Fagottini di Vitella ai Funghi Porcini

(Porcini Stuffed Veal Parcels)

ONION CONFIT

1/2 head of garlic, peeled and shaved
2 medium onions, peeled and shaved
1/3 cup (90 ml) extra virgin olive oil

MASHED POTATOES

2 pounds (900 g) Yukon Gold potatoes,
 peeled and quartered
6 cups (1.4 L) cold water
Sea salt
3/4 cup (175 ml) heavy cream
2 tablespoons (30 g) unsalted butter
Salt and freshly ground white pepper

VEAL FAGOTTINI

12 2-ounce (57 g) veal cutlets, pounded thin
1/4 pound (125 g) ham, diced
3 dry porcini mushrooms, soaked, rinsed and
 finely chopped (soaking liquid reserved)
2 tablespoons (30 g) chopped parsley
1/3 cup (85 g) shredded provolone cheese
Salt and freshly ground black pepper
2 tablespoons (30 ml) extra virgin olive oil

SAUCE

1/3 cup (90 ml) dry white wine
1 1/2 cups (360 ml) demi-glace (page 157)
2 fresh sage leaves
1 tablespoon (30 g) black truffle paste
Salt and freshly ground black pepper
3 tablespoons (45 ml) heavy cream

VEGETABLES

12 fresh asparagus spears, trimmed

GARNISH

Fresh sage

EQUIPMENT

2 small saucepans
Chef's knives and cutting board
Colander
Heavy sauté pan
Large pot
Ovenproof skillet
Plastic wrap
Potato ricer
Wooden spoon

Preheat oven to 320°F or 160°C.

For the onion confit, simmer garlic and onions in olive oil, in a small saucepan over medium heat for 20 minutes. Do not brown. Allow to cool. Cover and reserve.

For mashed potatoes, place potatoes into a pot filled with salted cold water. Bring to a boil and cook until potatoes are easily pierced with the tip of a knife, about 15 minutes. Drain potatoes using a colander and press potatoes through a potato ricer into a heated bowl. Stir in cream and butter. Adjust seasoning with salt and pepper. Set aside and keep warm.

For the veal filling, sauté 3 tablespoons (45 ml) onion confit with ham and porcini mushrooms in olive oil in a small sauté pan over medium heat for 3 minutes. Season with salt and pepper. Remove from heat and add chopped parsley. Let cool for 5 minutes then fold in provolone cheese.

Lay flattened veal cutlets on a clean work surface lined with plastic wrap so that the veal doesn't stick. Place two spoonfuls of ham mixture in the center of each scallopini (cutlet) and roll tightly, lengthwise, tucking in the ends to enclose the filling. Secure seams with wooden toothpicks if necessary.

In an ovenproof skillet over medium-high heat, warm olive oil and sear rolled veal on all sides. Place skillet in the oven and cook veal parcels for 5 minutes, uncovered. Remove from oven, cover with a piece of aluminum foil and keep warm.

For sauce, in a small saucepan over medium-high heat, warm 2 tablespoons (30 ml) of onion confit and sauté for 2 minutes. Deglaze with white wine, add demi-glace, sage leaves and reserved liquid from porcini mushrooms. Season with salt and pepper, reduce heat to low and simmer for 6 to 8 minutes or until mixture has reduced

by half. Add black truffle paste. Taste sauce and adjust seasoning with salt and pepper to taste.

Transfer 1/4 cup of the sauce into a small saucepan. Add heavy cream and simmer for 5 minutes. Keep both sauces warm.

Blanch asparagus in a pot of boiling salted water for 3 minutes.

Cut veal parcels at an angle.

Spoon mashed potatoes on warmed plates and top with halved veal parcels. Drizzle with creamy demi-glace. Add a couple spoonfuls of truffle demi-glace around the veal parcels. Garnish with asparagus and fresh sage.

Serves 6.

Difficulty 2.

Affogato al Caffé

MALAGA ICE CREAM
1/3 cup (85 g) raisins
1/4 cup (60 ml) quality dark rum
1/2 cup (115 g) powdered sugar
4 egg yolks
1 vanilla bean,
split and scraped to remove pulp
1 cup (240 ml) whole milk
1/2 cup (120 ml) heavy cream
Pinch of fine salt

PISTACHIO BISCOTTI
3/4 cup (175 g) unsalted pistachios
1/4 cup (60 g) unsalted butter,
softened at room temperature
2 eggs
1/2 cup (115 g) powdered sugar
1 teaspoon (5 ml) vanilla extract
1 3/4 cups (410 g) all-purpose flour
1/2 teaspoon (2.5 g) baking powder
Pinch of salt

NUT CROQUANT
1/2 teaspoon (2.5 ml) vegetable oil
1/2 cup (115 g) sugar
1/4 cup (60 ml) water
1/2 cup (115 g) slivered almonds

ESPRESSO SAUCE
1 tablespoon (15 g) coffee powder
1 3/4 cups (420 ml) heavy cream
3 egg yolks
1/4 cup (125 g) granulated sugar
2 tablespoons (30 ml) coffee liqueur

GARNISH
1/2 cup (120 ml) heavy cream,
whipped into soft peaks

EQUIPMENT
2 small saucepans
8-inch (20 cm) round cake pan
Chef's knife and cutting board
Cookie sheet
Fine sieve
Glass or stainless steel bowls
Handheld mixer
Ice cream maker
Ice cream scoop
Medium saucepan
Parchment paper or Silpat
Pastry brush
Plastic wrap
Spatula
Wire whisk
Wooden spoon

For Malaga ice cream, place raisins and rum in a plastic sandwich bag and macerate overnight in the fridge.

Place sugar, egg yolks and the pulp of the vanilla bean in a glass or stainless steel bowl and whisk for 6 to 7 minutes or until mixture is light and foamy.

In a saucepan over medium heat, warm milk, cream and salt for 3 minutes or until lukewarm. Whisk into egg mixture and stir well.

Pour combined mixtures back into saucepan and cook, over medium-low heat, stirring constantly for 5 to 6 minutes or until thickened. Do not allow mixture to boil.

Strain mixture through a sieve into a glass bowl. Let cool slightly before covering with a plastic wrap and chilling in the refrigerator for 2 hours.

Strain raisins, reserving the liquid. Whisk the leftover rum into the chilled ice cream mixture just before pouring it into the ice cream machine. Process as directed by manufacturer. When ice cream is almost ready, add in the macerated raisins

Transfer to a container. Cover and freeze.

For biscotti, preheat the oven to 350°F or 175°C.

Grease and lightly flour cake pan.

Lay pistachios in a single layer on a cookie sheet and bake for 8 to 10 minutes or until the nuts are lightly toasted. Remove from the oven and allow to cool.

Place butter in a large glass or stainless steel bowl and beat using a handheld electric mixer, set at medium speed, for 5 minutes or until light and fluffy.

With the mixer running, gradually add eggs, sugar, and vanilla; mix until creamed. Using a wooden spoon, fold in flour, baking powder, and salt. Mix until the dough is smooth, then stir in pistachios.

Pour mixture into cake pan and bake for 30 minutes or until the bottom of the log is light brown.

Meanwhile, make nut croquant by brushing the sides of a small saucepan with vegetable oil. Add sugar and water and cook over high heat, stirring occasionally with a wooden spoon. Once sugar mixture is boiling, cover and cook for 3 minutes. Uncover and cook the sugar until it turns a golden shade.

Remove from heat. Stir in almonds and pour on a cookie sheet lined with buttered parchment paper. Spread thin using a buttered spatula.

Let cool, then break into pieces.

For espresso sauce, combine coffee powder and heavy cream in a small saucepan and bring to a simmer over medium heat.

Whisk together egg yolks and sugar for 2 minutes in a glass bowl and slowly incorporate espresso mixture. Transfer into saucepan and cook over medium heat, stirring constantly until cream coats the back of a wooden spoon. Do not boil. Remove from heat. Pass through a fine sieve into a clean glass bowl and whisk in coffee liqueur. Cover and refrigerate for a couple hours.

Remove cake from the oven and let cool for 5 minutes.

For biscotti, place cake on a cutting board and gently slice diagonally into 1-inch thick slices. Arrange slices on a cookie sheet and bake for 10 minutes in total, flipping them over after 5 minutes on one side. Remove from the oven and let cool on a wire rack.

Place two scoops of Malaga ice cream into a chilled glass. Top with a piece of nut croquant, a biscotti and a rosette of whipped cream. Serve espresso sauce on the side.

Serves 6.

Difficulty 3.

Giovanni's Table

Cooking Basics

Chicken Stock

5 pounds (2.25 kg) chicken bones, including feet and neck,
or 2 roasted chicken carcasses
3 quarts (2.8 L) cold water
2 carrots, peeled and coarsely sliced
2 medium onions, coarsely chopped
2 stalks celery, coarsely chopped
1 leek, washed and cut into 1/2-inch (1.2 cm) chunks
2 cloves garlic, crushed
2 bay leaves
3 parsley sprigs
1/4 teaspoon (1.5 g) black peppercorns

Place chicken bones into a large pot and pour in cold water to cover by 2 inches (5 cm). Bring to a boil, regularly skimming off fat and froth that rise to the surface.

Once water is boiling, add remaining ingredients, reduce heat to low, cover and simmer for 2 1/2 to 3 hours, skimming occasionally.

Strain stock through a fine sieve lined with several layers of cheesecloth and refrigerate, uncovered, overnight.

Discard congealed layer of fat on the surface and strain once again into small containers or ice cube trays.

Use immediately or freeze it in small containers and use as needed.

Makes 2 1/2 quarts (2.4 L).

Fish Stock

BOUQUET GARNI

3 sprigs parsley
3 celery leaves
1 sprig thyme
1/4 teaspoon (1.5 g) black peppercorns
1 bay leaf

STOCK

2 tablespoons (30 ml) extra virgin olive oil
1 pound (450 g) fish bones and heads from any
saltwater fish, except salmon
1 carrot, peeled and coarsely sliced
1 shallot, coarsely chopped
1 small onion, coarsely chopped
1 stalk celery, coarsely chopped
1 leek, washed and cut into 1/2-inch (1.2 cm) chunks
1 clove garlic, crushed
1/4 cup (60 ml) dry white wine
5 cups (1.2 L) cold water

Prepare bouquet garni by wrapping parsley, celery, thyme, peppercorns and bay leaf inside a piece of cheesecloth and tying it with kitchen string.

In a saucepan over medium heat, warm oil and sauté fish bones and vegetables for 8 minutes. Add wine and stir, scraping the bottom of the pan. Add bouquet garni and enough water to completely cover fish. Bring to a boil, regularly skimming off fat and froth that rise to the surface. Reduce heat to low and simmer for 30 minutes.

Strain stock through a fine sieve lined with several layers of cheesecloth.

Use immediately or freeze it in small containers and use as needed.

Makes 1 quart (950 ml).

Vegetable Stock

2 tablespoons (30 ml) extra virgin olive oil
1 medium onion, coarsely chopped
1 leek, washed and cut into 1/2-inch (1.2 cm) chunks
1 stalk celery, coarsely chopped
1 turnip, peeled and coarsely chopped
2 carrots, peeled and coarsely chopped
2 tomatoes, peeled, seeded and chopped
1 clove garlic, crushed
3 sprigs parsley
1 sprig thyme
1 bay leaf
1/4 teaspoon (1.5 g) black peppercorns
5 cups (1.2 L) cold water

Heat oil in a stockpot over medium heat. Add vegetables and sauté for 10 minutes. Do not brown.

Add enough water to completely cover the vegetables. Reduce heat to low and simmer for 30 minutes.

Strain stock through a fine sieve lined with several layers of cheesecloth.

Use immediately or freeze it in small containers and use as needed.

Makes 1 quart (950 ml).

Beef Stock

4 pounds (1.8 kg) beef bones
1/2 pound (250 g) veal trimmings
1 onion, coarsely chopped
2 carrots, peeled and coarsely chopped
2 stalks celery, coarsely chopped
1 leek, washed and cut into 1/2-inch (1.2 cm) chunks
1 tablespoon (15 g) tomato paste
2 bay leaves
3 parsley sprigs
1/4 teaspoon (1.5 g) black peppercorns
2 1/2 quarts (2.4 L) cold water

Preheat oven to 400°F or 200°C.

Place beef bones, veal trimmings and onion in a roasting pan and roast uncovered for 1 hour or until bones are golden brown.

Transfer to a stockpot. Add remaining ingredients and pour in enough water to cover completely. Bring to a boil, uncovered, over medium heat. Reduce heat to low and simmer for 8 to 10 hours. Set aside and let cool.

Strain through a fine sieve lined with several layers of cheesecloth.

Use immediately or freeze it in small containers and use as needed.

Makes 2 quarts (1.8 L).

Brown Sauce

BOUQUET GARNI
3 sprigs parsley
3 celery leaves
1 sprig thyme
1/4 teaspoon (1.5 g) black peppercorns
1 bay leaf
SAUCE
4 tablespoons (60 g) unsalted butter
2 medium onions, diced
3 carrots, peeled and diced
3 stalks celery, diced
1/3 cup (90 g) all-purpose flour
3 tablespoons (45 g) tomato paste
4 cups (950 ml) beef stock
Salt and freshly ground black pepper

Prepare bouquet garni by wrapping parsley, celery, thyme, peppercorns and bay leaf inside a piece of cheesecloth and tying it with kitchen string.

In a medium saucepan over high heat, melt butter. Add onions, carrots and celery and sauté for 15 minutes until vegetables are turning golden brown.

Reduce heat to low and add flour, stirring continuously until flour turns brown. Add tomato paste and cook for another 2 minutes.

Gradually whisk in stock, add the bouquet garni and adjust seasoning with salt and pepper. Bring to a boil, regularly skimming off froth that rises to the surface. Simmer for about 45 minutes, until the sauce has reduced by half.

Strain through a fine sieve lined with several layers of cheesecloth.

Use immediately or freeze it in small containers and use as needed.

Makes 2 cups (480 ml).

Demi-Glace

1 cup (240 ml) brown sauce
1 cup (240 ml) beef stock
Salt and freshly ground black pepper

In a medium saucepan over medium heat, combine the stocks and simmer for about 30 minutes, until reduced by half.

Strain through a fine sieve lined with several layers of cheesecloth. Adjust seasoning with salt and pepper.

Use demi-glace immediately or freeze it in small containers and use as needed.

Makes 1 cup (240 ml).

Simple Syrup

1/4 cup (60 g) granulated sugar
1/4 cup (60 ml) water

Prepare syrup by mixing all ingredients in a small saucepan and boiling until sugar is melted, or about 5 minutes. Remove from heat and allow cooling. Transfer into a glass bottle and refrigerate. Simple syrup will keep for 2 to 3 weeks in the refrigerator.

Cooking Terms

AL DENTE: Italian for "to the tooth" and is used to describe a food that is cooked until it gives a slight resistance when one bites into it.

BLANCHING: Cooking a food very briefly and partially in boiling water or hot fat as part of a combination cooking method. Usually used to loosen peels from vegetables and fruits.

BLENDING: A mixing method in which two or more ingredients are combined until they are evenly distributed; a spoon, rubber spatula, whisk or electric mixer with its paddle attachment can be used.

BOIL: To cook in water or other liquid at an approximate temperature of 212°F or 100°C at sea level.

BOUQUET GARNI: A blend of herbs and vegetables tied in a bundle with twine and used to flavor stocks, soups, sauces and stews.

BROIL: To cook by heat radiating from an overhead source.

CARAMELIZE: Fruits and vegetables with natural sugars can be caramelized by sautéing, roasting or grilling, giving them a sweet flavor and golden glaze.

CHIFFONADE: To slice into thin strips or shreds.

CLARIFIED BUTTER: Purified butterfat; the butter is melted and water and milk solids are removed: also known as drawn butter.

CONCASSÉ: To chop coarsely.

DEGLAZE: To swirl or stir a liquid like wine or stock in a pan to dissolve cooked food particles remaining on the bottom, using the mixture as the base for the sauce.

DEGREASE: To skim the fat from the top of a liquid.

DICE: To cut food into cubes.

DREDGE: To coat food with flour, breadcrumbs or cornmeal before frying.

FLAMBÉ: Pour warmed spirits such as brandy, whisky or rum over foods such as fruits or meat and then ignite it.

FOLD: To combine a light ingredient like egg whites with a much heavier mixture like whipped cream.

FRY: To cook in hot fat.

GELATIN: A colorless, odorless and flavorless mixture of proteins made from animal bones, connective tissues and certain algae; when dissolved in warm liquid it forms a jelly-like substance used as a thickener for desserts, cold soups and certain sauces.

GRILL: Cooking in which the heat source is located beneath the rack on which the food is placed.

JULIENNE: Foods cut into matchstick shapes.

MACERATE: Soaking fruits in liquid, such as brandy or other alcoholic ingredients, so they absorb that flavor. Macerate can also be fruits sprinkled with sugar, which draws out the natural juices of the fruit, creating a syrup.

MARINADE: A seasoned liquid in which raw foods are soaked or coated to absorb flavors and/or become tender before cooking.

MINCE: To cut or chop a food finely.

MONTER: To finish a sauce by swirling or whisking in butter until it is melted.

PAN-BROIL: To cook food uncovered and without fat.

PAN-FRY: To cook food in a moderate amount of hot fat, uncovered.

POACH: To gently cook food submerged in a simmering liquid.

PURÉE: To process food to achieve a smooth pulp.

REDUCE: To cook by simmering a liquid until the quantity decreases by evaporation.

REFRESH: The process of submerging food (usually vegetables) in cold water to cool it quickly and prevent further cooking.

SEAR: To brown a food quickly over high heat.

SEASON: Adding flavor to foods. Season can also mean to coat the surface of a new pot or pan with vegetable oil and place in a hot oven for about 1 hour. As the oil burns off, the carbon residue fills in the small pits and groves of the pan's surface making a smooth finish that helps prevent food from sticking.

SIMMER: To maintain the temperature of a liquid just below the boiling point.

STIR-FRY: To cook food over high heat with little fat while stirring constantly and briskly.

Index

This cookbook is the latest example of our ongoing commitment and relentless pursuit by Royal Caribbean International's Culinary, Beverage and Restaurant Operations teams to enhance the experience of our valued guests, by providing them with the highest level of distinctive culinary quality and innovation.

The creation of *Carte du Jour 2nd Edition* was made possible with the support of:
Richard Fain, Chairman and CEO of Royal Caribbean Cruises, Ltd;
Adam Goldstein, President and CEO of Royal Caribbean International and
Lisa Lutoff-Perlo, Executive Vice President, Operations, Royal Caribbean International

Additional Appreciation to:
Ken Taylor, AVP Food & Beverage Operations,
Josef Jungwirth, Director of Fleet Culinary Operations,
Bob Midyette, Director of Fleet Beverage Operations,
Naomi Celaire-Hattema, Manager of Beverage Operations,
Marco Marrama, Senior Executive Chef,
Maureen "Molly" Brandt, Chef de Cuisine, 150 Central Park, Allure of the Seas
Stefan Brueggeman, Corporate Pastry Chef,
Travis Kamiyama, Chef Consultant Izumi and
Tad Ware & Company Publishing and Photography team

Author:
Corinne Lewis, Manager F&B Business Operations & Development, authored and coordinated
Savor^{sm}, *Carte du Jour* and *Cupcakes and Scoops* cookbook collections.